ANDERTON FOR ORDERS

ANDERTON FOR ORDERS

*memoirs of a canal boatman
in the early 1950s*

by

Tom   Foxon

B

M & M BALDWIN
Cleobury Mortimer, Shropshire
1997

Bibliographic Note

This book was first published by J. M. Pearson & Associates in 1988. This new edition contains the entire text and illustrations from the first edition, although the illustrations in the first edition were in colour. No changes have been made to the text, but the illustrations have been repositioned, and an index has been added.

Publishers' Acknowledgements

We are grateful to J. M. Pearson & Associates for their kind permission to reprint this book, and to Brian Collings for allowing us to use his illustrations.

Cover designed by David Miller

Text © Tom Foxon, 1988
Illustrations © Brian Collings 1988, 1997

ISBN 0 947712 33 X

British Library Cataloguing in Publication Data
A catalogue record is available from the British Library.

Published by M & M Baldwin
24 High Street, Cleobury Mortimer, Kidderminster DY14 8BY

Printed by MFP Design & Print
Longford Trading Estate, Thomas Street, Stretford, Manchester M32 0JT

CONTENTS

CHAPTER ONE

INTRODUCTION TO THE CUT

·

I n adventure stories of old, boys used to run away to sea, returning, many years later, to their aged parents, loaded down with wealth and honours. The desire to make a complete break with the environment in which one has been brought up is still a common urge, though opportunities for doing so have become fewer over the years. Even in my own youth, nobody could run away to sea unless they had first managed to get hold of a Union Card; but a trickle of boys could and did, as they have done ever since the canals were built, leave their conventional life ashore for a vastly different existence on The Cut.

Not that canals had any particular attraction for me as a child. We lived near enough to the Grand Union Canal at Heston for the sight of boats and barges to be commonplace. Romantic sea stories I could read in plenty, but the picturesque life of the canal boatman had yet to be revealed to the outside world by L.T.C. Rolt and Susan Woolfit. For me, romance was to be found in the flailing coupling rods and screaming whistles of the Great Western expresses as they tore through Southall station; though in between planning a career as an engine driver, I gave occasional consideration to the imposing, white-capped pilots of Salter's Thames steamers. In those days, of course, they were real steamers and one could peep down the engine-room hatch and watch a poem of gleaming paint and shiny brass and steel at work.

Fired by the tales of one of my uncles, who worked for Bristol Tramways, I also gave thought to the possible enjoyment which might be derived from being in command of one of the huge, groaning monsters, with their polished brass controls on which we often rode in Southall or Hounslow. Great was my annoyance when these impressive vehicles were replaced by trolleybuses.

During the war, we went to live in Buckinghamshire, and it was while I was at school there that canals began to interest me. This came about when, in my school atlas, I came across a map of the waterway system. For the first time it was borne upon me that a canal was not just a vague stretch of water, but actually started somewhere and went to somewhere else. To me, the discovery that a whole network of waterways covered the country, was a revelation. That a canal should connect the Kennet and the Avon or penetrate to Oxford (I had been to Oxford without ever realising that there was a canal there) seized my imagination. From that day I was hooked on the idea of canals, and lost no opportunity to seek them out. My atlas must have been very out of date as it showed the Wilts & Berks Canal; the next time I stayed with relations at Didcot, I cycled out to find it, only to be disappointed by discovering a muddy ditch.

When, shortly afterwards, we moved to Reading, I not only started to explore the local waterways but also began to comb the library shelves for books on the subject. Surprisingly, for there was very little interest in inland waterways in the years 1946/7, Reading Library stocked a variety of books on the subject, all of which I avidly devoured. There was Thacker on the Thames and Kennet, Cadbury and Pratt on canal economics, Bliss and Lloyd to set my imagination roaming as I followed their journeys by canoe and motor cruiser. But the three books that particularly interested me were Susan Woolfit's "Idle Women", Emma Smith's "Maiden's Trip" and L. T. C. Rolt's "Narrow Boat". The first two introduced me to canal boats, boatmen and the techniques of working, while I was just at the age to absorb the combination of romance and idealism in "Narrow Boat". It is a book that has affected my philosophy ever since.

While I lived at Reading, I spent many hours on the towpath of the Kennet. The deserted, reedy channel, the crumbling red brick bridges and the lonely locks were a welcome escape from the pressures of home and school. I feel sorry for any adolescent of a solitary disposition today, now that most of the lonely places near to towns have disappeared under housing or industrial estates, have been obliterated by road works or been converted into dreary public open spaces. In my explorations of the Kennet, I longed to come across a boat, but I was to be disappointed until, one day, I encountered a working narrow boat called *Westminster* tied up at the wharf below County Lock. There was no one aboard and I was not to know, at that time, that she had just completed an epic voyage with ten tons of grain from Avonmouth to Newbury.

The following year, 1948, I left school and started work and it was around then that I discovered the Inland Waterways Association which I joined. I was also able to buy a new bike which extended my range of canal exploration. Two such expeditions stand out in my mind. The first was to Uxbridge, where I found a canal alive with traffic. Boatbuilders were busy at Fellows, Morton's dockyard and boats were unloading coal at the Uxbridge Trading Estate. A horse drawn barge was coming down empty from Denham and other barges were moored at the numerous wharves. I discovered George and Sonia Smith, whom I had seen mentioned in the I W A Bulletin, unloading at Uxbridge Power Station with their boats, *Cairo* and *Warwick*. While I was talking to George, a fleet of a dozen loaded Joshers came past, forging uphill at a great rate, and I watched, fascinated, as pair after pair passed me at intervals of about five minutes.

My visit to Oxford was quite different. Isis Lock, by which the Oxford Canal enters the Thames, was the first narrow lock I had seen; it appeared so small that I marvelled that a canal boat could use it. The wharves were deserted as I cycled up the towpath. The day was so fine and the canal so enticing that I was reluctant to turn back, and I did not, in fact, retrace my footsteps until I reached Gibraltar Lock at Enslow. I was disappointed not to see any boats, especially as, a few weeks later, a friend reported seeing two S. E. Barlow's at Juxon St. Wharf.

After my visit to Oxford, I became interested in getting a job connected with canals. At the time it never occurred to me to actually work on a boat; what I had in mind was something on the administrative side. I made many enquiries but with no success; finally it occurred to me to ask the I W A to mention me in their "Bulletin" in the hope that one of their canal carrier members might offer me a job.

My advert duly appeared, and, not long afterwards, a letter arrived which was to change the entire course of my life. It came from a Mr. John Knill and offered me a job as a trainee mate on his boats. My first reaction was that this was not what I was seeking; this was the 1940's, a period when most young people tended to be more conservative in their choice of employment than was later to become the case. My whole upbringing had brainwashed me into believing that a clerical occupation was not only more desirable than a manual one but was also the one to which I was most suited. However, after a few days consideration I had second thoughts.

For the last eighteen months I had crept reluctantly to work at the local office of one of our most well known Insurance Companies.

Here my painfully acquired School Certificate was put to good use filling inkwells and hunting for mislaid files. My salary was the princely sum of £2.10 shillings per week of which I was allowed to retain the shillings. No hint of laughter or happiness penetrated this doleful hall of commerce. High on his dais, the Chief Clerk was lord of all he surveyed. Beneath his frosty gaze, the serried ranks of minions, forbidden even to smoke, dared not raise their eyes from their work for fear of incurring his displeasure. The salaries were said to be the lowest in the Insurance industry, and membership of a Union, if discovered, meant that all hopes of promotion could be forgotten.

In the same department as myself worked an old man who had once been an Inspector. An Inspector was a sort of minor deity, four of whom descended on us once a month and were actually received in the Holy of Holies where dwelt the Branch Manager. Like Lucifer, he had fallen from grace and had been despatched to the nether regions for some obscure sexual peccadillo. His fate was only alluded to in hushed tones. "Poor old Smith – he got into trouble over a woman, you know."

When I look back on my thankfully short experience of office life in the late 1940's, I am surprised that those younger members of the staff who had not long emerged from active service in the war should have put up with such low pay and such a miserable environment; but perhaps they didn't tolerate the situation for long as I am assured that such places as I describe are now no more than an unpleasant memory.

There being ample incentive, I thought, to change my lifestyle, I replied to John Knill expressing interest, and he travelled over to Reading to see me. Over lunch, he explained the working conditions on the cut (long hours and very dirty) and offered me a job at £1 per week all found, plus 15 shillings per trip, which was more than double my present disposable income.

John was then aged 37 and had bought a pair of canal boats on leaving the Navy, which he worked on sub-contract to British Waterways. At that time he was without any crew and proposed, for the time being, to work his motor boat, *Columba*, as a two handed single motor until he could make up a crew of three to work the pair. When we parted it had been arranged that, having worked out my notice, I should travel up to Braunston where his boats were moored.

My parents were far from pleased when I announced my decision, considering that their social standing would be lowered when it became known that their son had become a 'bargee'; but when my intentions became known in the typing pool I became, all at once, a romantic figure and was able to date a young lady who had, up till then, turned her nose up at the office boy. Having rarely been away from home before and with virtually no experience of life, I had my own misgivings, but my mind was made up. The next week went by on leaden wings, until Friday afternoon came and I was able to walk out of the office door for the last time.

Standing on the chilly platform of Reading West station that January afternoon in 1950, I found my misgivings fast disappearing in the anticipation of the journey before me. In those days, any journey beyond one's immediate environment was an adventure. How much less fortunate are today's teenagers, for most of whom travelling is commonplace and who, even if they are going somewhere new, have quite possibly seen their destination depicted on television or described and photographed at length. In 1950, each town and city retained its distinctive character, in most cases lost today under the uniformity of shopping precinct and urban motorway. As for rural areas, the difficulties of travel before the era of mass car ownership gave them an air of unfrequented remoteness long since gone.

The village to which I was bound, Braunston, in Warwickshire, was, to me as mysterious a destination as Timbuctoo. Of recent years it has been so much written about and photographed that any one interested in canals can be quite familiar with it without actually going there. From the brief references to it in the canal literature of the day, unaccompanied as they were by photographs, I found it hard to envisage; therefore, my anticipation was the keener and my arrival there the more exciting.

The rattle of signal wires was followed by the grimy shape of a "King Arthur" locomotive, as the South Coast to Wolverhampton express rumbled into the platform. It was very lightly patronised and I had a compartment to myself all the way. Up the familiar Thames Valley we sped, the rhythm of wheels on rail-joints clicking off the miles. I got out of the train at Oxford and walked up to the head of the platform to watch our Southern engine being replaced by a Western "Castle", a familiar friend from my engine spotting days. For much of the way beyond Oxford the railway runs close to the Oxford Canal and indeed crosses it in several places. I moved from side to side of my compartment in order to see as much of it as possible. Hampton Gay, once the scene of a dreadful accident; Heyford Wharf, in an afternoon dream of the boats that no longer came; and the sharp turn by Little Bourton, with drinking cattle so far out in the canal as to make me wonder if there was really sufficient depth of water for boats to navigate. That afternoon I saw no boat disturb these silent waters where only the herons stood guard, stolidly ignoring our screaming whistle and clattering wheels. An early winter dusk was falling as the train left Banbury and it was already dark as we drew into Leamington.

John Knill was waiting for me on the platform and we had time for a cup of tea before boarding the Braunston train at the adjoining London Midland station. Soon we were winding slowly across the night-shrouded Midland plain, our journey punctuated by stops at stations with intriguing names like Long Itchington, Napton & Stockton, and Flecknoe, the latter being literally in the middle of nowhere. Wisps of steam rose into the cold night air as we alighted at the feebly lit platform of Braunston station. We walked out onto the road and turned left. Opposite was a pub and a collection of sheds, beyond which we turned right onto the towpath of a canal arm. On the other side of the canal were more shedlike buildings and the shape of boats could be dimly perceived through the dark. Stars burnt brightly in the winter sky and the quietness was almost tangible. *Columba* was moored alongside the towpath.

John unlocked the cabin and I stepped aboard, finding myself on a small platform at the stern of the boat, from which projected the Z shaped curve of the rudder head. Below, in the cabin, John had switched on the light. I was advised to enter backwards, and did so, finding a foothold on the coal box. Sitting down on a seat which ran the full length of the cabin looking forwards, I took stock of my surroundings. Opposite, a small coal range gleamed with blacklead as John urged it into life. To its right was a cupboard, the front of which, I discovered, let down to form a table. Beyond was another, larger flap with a small cupboard above and a drawer beneath. This let down to form a bed athwart the cabin, which, in this type of boat, was separated from the engine room (or engine-hole in boating parlance) by a solid bulkhead. The whole effect was very cosy and, despite the cabin being only about eight feet long, gave no impression of being cramped.

As we sat talking and eating a meal of sausages and beans, we heard the distant beat of an engine and *Columba* started to move as the water in the arm responded to the approach of a pair of boats. "That's a

Bolinder", said John and went on to explain that the two commonest types of engine on the cut were Bolinders and Nationals and that *Columba* was equipped with the latter. I stood on the coal box and looked out of the cabin slide to see the long, low-laden shapes framed by the cast iron bridge which spanned the arm. John told me that when we left Braunston we would be bound for Middlewich in Cheshire to load salt for Newbury on the Kennet & Avon Canal. More engines were heard as boat after boat arrived and tied up for the night, the disturbance of the water setting us gently moving.

Columba was unusual in that she had an extra cabin forward of the engine hole. This was John's bedroom and office. He showed me how to let down the flap and make the bed in the back cabin, and, having revealed the sanitary arrangements – "There's a bucket in the engine-hole and if nature calls in the night just use the canal" – he wished me goodnight and retired to his den. I put my head outside and had a final look round before pulling the slide over and going to bed.

Excitement, and being in a strange bed, caused me to sleep less well than usual. I got up when it grew light, stowed away the bedding and put up the flap of the bed-hole. The next task was to rake the ashes out of the range and get the fire going. I was soon joined by John who showed me how to operate the Primus stove. "The most essential bit of equipment on the boat" was his description of it and indeed it was an invaluable asset, not only for producing that early morning cuppa without which no boatman's day can start, but for warming up the cabin and cooking when the range wasn't in use.

We had breakfast and I was given a list of rations and stores to get from the village. It was one of those bright, windless, frosty mornings, an ideal start for my first day on the canals. I crossed the side-bridge over the arm and walked up the towpath of the main line, crossing the canal at the first bridge and following a steep path up the green hillside to the village which was strung out on top of a ridge on the opposite side of the valley from the railway station and the boatyard. On my return, I found that we would not be leaving until midday, as John had to interview a prospective mate, so we polished the brasses and had a stroll round the dockyard.

Braunston Dock belonged to the Samuel Barlow Coal Co. Ltd., usually referred to as the 'Limited' to distinguish it from another carrier called S. E. Barlow. My overwhelming impression of the dock on that occasion was the large number of boats lying around. Immediately across the arm from us lay the oiling-up (refuelling) berth.

On the left of this was the entrance to a lagoon up which were a number of boats, some waiting repair or Captains, others obviously left there to rot quietly away. To the right of the oil berth was a slip on which lay a partially built new wooden boat. Next to the slip was the fitting shop with the newly docked *Rocket* moored alongside while overall clad figures did mysterious things inside her engine-hole. In 1950, single cylinder Bolinders and Petters predominated in the Barlow fleet. They had, however, installed 2-cylinder Gardners (a highly regarded engine) and Rustons in a few boats and in the years to come were to replace many more of their older engines with Listers and Armstrongs.

Two dry docks were next, on one of which a painter was applying the distinctive Barlow livery to the cabin side of the *Cylgate*. Next to the dry docks was the office and, spanning the extreme end of the arm, an old transhipment shed, a relic from the days when this was a Fellows, Morton & Clayton depot and goods were transhipped between steamers, which ran between Brentford and Braunston, and horse boats which collected and delivered goods between Braunston and various parts of the Midlands. More boats lay under the transhipment shed, none of which looked as though it had been used for a long time. The main gate was to the left of this shed and separated it from the "Ship" public house. Near the gate was an old enamel sign advertising "Daily Steamboat Services to London". Then came the entrance to the towpath where we were tied alongside a range of buildings which had contained the old FMC stables.

After lunch we were ready to leave and I was introduced to our National engine. First of all, a short metal strip, curved at one end, had to be inserted in the fuel pump and worked up and down to prime the engine. The decompression lever, known as the lifter, was raised and I was instructed to drop it when told. John inserted the starting handle, wound vigorously and, when sufficient momentum had been obtained, told me to drop the lifter. With a cough and a splutter the squat green monster burst into life.

I went forward and let go the bow-rope, which boatmen always call the fore-string. John let go the stern string, put the engine into forward gear and the boat slid forward. There is a sharp turn out of the arm onto the main line. The tiller was put hard over, the throttle opened, and round we went to the accompaniment of an impressive spray of water as the rudder forced the wash out sideways under the counter. Almost immediately we came to a triangular junction and turned right onto the Oxford Canal, northbound. The canal wound a tortuous way through damp green pastures, former ridge and furrow cultivation being clearly evident. On our right the ground rose towards a low range of hills, while the valley of the Leam lay on our left. We were in remote countryside with few signs of life except for sheep. Every now and then we would meet a pair of boats, all of which were loaded with coal. Each steerer would nod gravely and say, "How d'ye do". The women would often be knitting or peeling potatoes as they leant against the great, curved tillers, making the heavy task of steering a butty seem deceptively easy.

After a while we came to the stretch of canal known as Barby Straight and I was allowed to take the tiller for the first time. I was surprised at the pressure that had to be exerted to move the tiller while underway as I had previously experimented with it when we were tied up. There were two controls, the throttle, operated by a small handle rather like that on a motor lawn-mower, and the forward and reverse gear operated by a wheel about 6" in diameter. Both were positioned under the cabin roof in front of the door-hole. The gear wheel was well situated to give you a nasty crack on the head as you climbed out of the cabin. It could also remove the skin from your knuckles when you tried to turn it especially as it often had to be given a sharp jerk to get it into or out of gear. I was not allowed to steer for very long on the first few days but later, when I was doing a lot of steering, I would find my arm and shoulder muscles aching at the end of the day until I got used to it. Having negotiated a couple of bridge-holes successfully, I was given a windlass and sent ahead to prepare Hillmorton locks. I had spent many hours helping the lock-keeper at Caversham on the Thames and thought I knew all about locks; but finding myself alone and confronted by my first canal lock I experienced a moment of panic and had to force myself to remember what to do first. I shut the bottom gates, lowered the bottom paddles and raised those at the top. The lock was ready as *Columba* came in sight. There was a flurry of water as she went astern. John left her ticking over in gear to hold her down against the bottom gates while he shut the top gate and I drew the bottom paddles before running down to the next lock. I already knew that you always ran when working locks although it took me some time to acquire the boatmans knack of whipping up the paddles like lightning.

On the subject of windlasses, there were three sizes, the one with the largest square fitting the paddle spindles on the Grand Union

Canal, the smallest for use on the Trent Mersey and the intermediate size for use elsewhere. A good windlass was highly prized, the best ones being made at a small town on the Trent Mersey Canal and known as "Wheelock" windlasses. These could be identified by a pipe shaped mark on the shank. Some boatmen had their windlasses chromed. There were several methods of carrying a windlass. It could be tucked through your belt, handle downwards and the eye preventing it from slipping through or carried in a V shaped fashion, tucked in the belt either across your stomach or behind your back. After some experimentation I came to prefer carrying it over the shoulder, held in place by my jacket. The handle came readily to hand and it was less likely to slip and fall in the cut. This was bound to happen occasionally and the more crafty boatmen carried a magnet and a rake and could recover his own and other peoples windlasses, of which the latter commanded a ready sale. We once lost a T&M sized Wheelock windlass on *Columba* and made many fruitless enquiries of lock-keepers in case we had left it behind somewhere; it was a pleasant surprise to find it eventually in the engine hole bilges.

Windlasses could have other uses besides drawing paddles. They were reputed to be used in fights between boatmen. If one believed all the old boatmen's tales, very little work could have been done on the canal because they spent most of their time fighting. When I worked on the cut nobody seemed very pugnacious. I did hear of one boatman striking another on Barlow's dock – he was sacked on the spot. Evidently modern management disapproved of this traditional sport! Nevertheless you still heard rumours that so and so was wont to lurk behind bridgeholes and leap out and attack his enemies with a windlass. I found nearly all boatmen to be very easy going although some of the women could be a bit fearsome and many were certainly sharp-tongued. Perhaps they hankered for the days when every lockside ran red with gore, but it was noticeable that when they started arguing the men would unobtrusively make themselves scarce.

It was after we had left Hillmorton that I encountered my first horse-drawn boat, one of S.E. Barlow's 'Joey' boats bound for the Co-op wharf up the Rugby Arm. We carried on, through the short tunnel at Newbold, round the bends by All Oaks Wood, through Stretton Stop, waving to the drivers of trains on the nearby West Coast main line, and round the sharp and mud-encumbered turn at Ansty. Dusk was beginning to soften the landscape as the first spoil heaps of the Warwickshire coal field appeared on our left at Binley, as strange and romantic to me as Egyptian pyramids. It was dark when we reached Tushes Bridge, where a few pairs of boats were already tied up for the night. Passing through the tangle of gantries, overhead conveyors and steaming cooling towers that was Longford Power Station, with its queue of boats waiting to unload, we rounded a sharp left hand turn and found ourselves in a narrow lane of water with boats moored on both sides. We pulled into the side and tied up. This was Sutton's Stop, nerve centre of the Warwickshire coal traffic and reputed mecca of all boatmen. Certainly there were enough boats tied up here both loaded and empty. As we walked up the towpath to find George and Sonia Smith who were tied up a little ahead of us, a pair of Harvey Taylor's (a small general carrier from Aylesbury) pulled out of the lock, the Bolinder engine giving out a steady beat as they slid slowly between the lines of boats.

Welcoming lamplight shone from *Warwick's* cabin doors as we knocked on the cabin side and were invited aboard. Brasses gleamed and the boatmen's traditional decoration of lace edged hanging-up plates and white crochetwork surrounded us. Sonia made a pot of tea and produced some hot pies from the oven. George recognised me from our encounter at Uxbridge. "So you've come to work on the dirty old coal boats then", he remarked. "Well, it may not be a very good job but there's some good men on it". We discussed the state of trade. Morale was far from good at that time, following the recent liquidation of Fellows, Morton & Clayton and the imposition of a loading surcharge by the National Coal Board on all coal carried by boat. I was fascinated by the talk of boats and boating and the rest of the evening passed all too quickly. Soon it was time to say "Goodnight". Back again in *Columba's* warm, cosy cabin, where I now felt completely at home, I soon fell asleep to the gentle lapping of water against her hull.

CHAPTER TWO

COAL TO BIRMINGHAM

The clatter of watercans as kettles were filled, and the sound of engines being persuaded into life woke me next morning. We were able to have a leisurely breakfast as John wanted to call at the Boat Control Office, a wooden hut situated by the junction of the Coventry and Oxford canals, in order to fix a cargo for part of the journey north. The office opened at 9 o'clock and ten minutes before this a small group of boatmen were assembled outside waiting for their orders. At this time about nine colliery loading points on the Coventry and Ashby canals came within the scope of the Boat Control Scheme, as did the craft of both British Waterways and all the private carriers wishing to load in the Warwickshire Coalfield. It was not only necessary to ensure that the correct craft were despatched to load at the appropriate place, to enable the many different coal contracts to be fulfilled, but also to distribute the boats daily in accordance with each colliery's ability to load them. The correct grades and quantities of coal required were then arranged with the collieries. A small amount of stone traffic was also dealt with and cash advances to the boatmen could be made if necessary. Boats entering the coalfield at the 'Bottom End' reported to S. E. Barlow's office at Glascote (Tamworth) which liaised with the Boat Control Office. There was also a Toll Office at Sutton's , which was shortly to be closed down. "The Greyhound" pub and its shop comprised the rest of the commercial activities here; it also supplied fuel, lubricating oil and stabling.

While John was in the office I was busy cleaning up the boat. Around me was constant movement as people hurried between boats, shop, water tap and Control Office. Every now and then an empty pair of boats would receive its order and depart. A small tug, the *Enterprise*, locked through with a train of loaded Joey-boats, while I got a fleeting glimpse of an empty horse-boat bound northwards from the direction of Coventry and travelling at a great rate. The white cloud of condensate from the nearby cooling towers precipitated a fine rain and there was an occasional acrid whiff from the nearby Courtauld's tip. The waste products of the rayon industry are of a particularly unpleasant nature.

"Baddesley for Birmingham!" John told me when he returned. We untied, went through the Stop Lock with its six-inch difference in level, and made a sharp right-hand turn onto the Coventry Canal, passing immediately through a 'stop place'; a narrowing of the canal where boats have their loads gauged in order to calculate the tonnage on board. The bright frosty weather had given way to grey skies but it was mild and remained windless. To our left lay the defunct remains of coal mining activity around Exhall; on our right we passed the unloading wharf for Courtauld's tip. Soon we rounded a sharp bend and could see coal being shovelled into boats through the pall of dust which covered the Newdegate Arm. A women in a figure-hugging yellow sweater was shafting a boat out into the main line while a small girl vigorously attacked its grimy paintwork with a large mop. Going along Bedworth Straight, John enlarged upon our orders. Baddesley Colliery Basin was above the sixth lock of the Atherstone flight and our destination was a firm called Bellis & Morcom on the Icknield Port Road Loop of the BCN. The job was a sub-contract for S.E. Barlow.

As we wound our way through the fields beyond Marston Junction we met the first boats of the day from Atherstone; two pairs of Joshers, recognisable in the distance by their distinctive cocked up fore-ends. They were loaded nearly to the gunwhales and were all neatly sheeted up. I asked John what they were likely to be carrying and was surprised to be told that it was coal. The full sheeting up was, it appeared, a determination on the part of the boatmen to cling to the old Josher 'style' despite nationalisation. FMC had been a merchandise carrier and its boats had rarely carried coal. Now its fleet had been incorporated into the mixed coal and merchandise operation of the former Grand Union Canal Carrying Co. The demise of Fellows, Morton & Clayton was a traumatic experience for canal people. The ubiquitous maroon, green and yellow boats of this historic firm, with its headquarters at the heart of the canal system in Birmingham and its tentacles spreading out to connect the Midlands with the Thames, Trent and Mersey had become a sight so longstanding and familiar that it was almost unthinkable that it should disappear. But the smart livery was replaced by drab yellow and blue paint, many of the depots were sold off and much of the traffic immediately disappeared. "You hardly ever saw an empty Josher" bemoaned John speaking of the recent past.

We emerged from a bridge-hole to pass the almost grotto-like entrance to the Griff Arm, embowered in the woods of Griff Hollow, and almost immediately entered the outskirts of Nuneaton. Now the canal began to get shallow and the reason for this was soon evident as we passed the disused chutes of Judkin's Quarry and observed the red stream of quarry tailings being discharged into the canal. One of the 'bridges-lengths' around here gives the strange impression that you are going downhill. Quarrying activity was to be seen along the granite ridge which lies to the west of the Coventry Canal between Nuneaton and Mancetter. At one time the carriage of roadstone on the canal had been an important traffic, the road authorities ordering their supplies in summer when the coal trade was slack. It was carried by canal not only from this area but also from Mountsorrel on the River Soar and from Rowley Regis (the famous Rowley Rag) on the BCN. The loss of this summer roadstone traffic must have been one reason why so little domestic coal was now carried by canal but coal required for industrial processes is, of course, consumed in more regular quantities all the year round, and a balancing summer traffic is not so essential.

The stone used to be landed at numerous small wharves along the canal system, having to be unloaded by shovel and wheelbarrow and then shovelled up into lorries as required. Once the age of the motor lorry had arrived those concerned with this traffic should have discontinued this expensive and time wasting exercise and equipped one wharf in each area with means to unload boats into hoppers from which lorries could help themselves as and when the stone was needed. For example, the three stone wharves at Heyford, Enslow, and Kidlington, all in a distance of only seven miles could have been replaced by one. John Knill tried to recover the Oxford County Council roadstone traffic in 1954 but ran into difficulties as the contract also involved factoring the stone. Three years later Willow Wren moved a few trial loads to Heyford and Kidlington, using a mobile crane for discharging, but no regular contract resulted. Meanwhile the last remnant of the stone trade was an occasional cargo from Griff, Mountsorrel or Mancetter to a plant at West Drayton.

Not that the roadstone trade was universally popular with boatmen. Granite is very heavy relative to its bulk and carriers with old wooden boats were worried about the strain put on their craft, the weight tending to pull the sides inwards. It is also a dead weight on the shovel making unloading by this method even harder work than shovelling coal; and many of the landings, particularly on the Grand Junction Canal, were so shallow and the boats lay so far off that the stone had to be wheeled out on planks. Rose Skinner once summed up the stone trade in a nutshell. "It was whip and windlass all the way going and shovel and barrow when you got there." We shall meet Rose later on in this story.

There is a pleasant mooring at Mancetter with a canalside pub and from there to the top lock of Atherstone the canal winds through delightful rolling parkland. The approach to Atherstone is preceeded by a short stretch lined with houses after which you pass under a bridge to emerge in a typical canal scene. In front lay the open gate of the top lock, from which was emerging the brightly painted deck-board of a Coventry bound Cowburn & Cowpar motor-boat. On our left a pair of British Waterways boats were being loaded with coal brought by road from Orchard Colliery, while on the opposite side of the canal a side bridge of mellow red brick gave entrance to a reed filled basin surrounded by graceful Georgian warehouses. On the towpath an assortment of pulleys and rollers was provided to enable horses to get some way on ascending boats before having to slacken their lines to go over the side bridge, the canal here being widened to enable boats to wind.

The Cowpar's captain held up six fingers to indicate that he had made ready all the locks as far as Baddesley and we dropped down them in short order. After drawing the bottom paddles at each lock I was told to get back on the boat and accelerate her out of the lock after John had opened the bottom gates, although I was not, as yet, allowed to steer into the locks. We passed a small gasworks and a wharf with an old wooden jibbed crane where boats formerly unloaded grain for a mill, the boat horses being used to provide power to hoist up the bags. At one time a great deal of grain was moved from London to all parts of the Midlands by canal, the task of transhipping and stowing the two hundredweight bags being particularly arduous. This was a common and useful back loading for coal boats.

By around the end of the 19th century, the milling industry was tending more and more to site itself either at the ports or at inland locations where imported grain could be cheaply transported by river barge. The 1906 mills at Ellesmere Port and Worcester and those of 1898 at Tewkesbury are examples, all of which had the facility for despatching flour to the industrial Midlands by narrow canal boat. After the Second World War the industry tended to concentrate in fewer and larger units, still retaining, in some cases, barge transport for the raw material. The whole pattern of this trade was disrupted in the 1980s by a massive reduction in the use of imported grain and concentration of such of the traffic as remained at Tilbury and Seaforth (Liverpool). Severn grain barges for example, prevented by lack of an adequate inland waterway system from loading anywhere other than at the Bristol Channel ports, became redundant. Most grain for milling is now home-grown and transported by lorry.

In the small country town where I live, the local mill was enlarged (other local mills being closed) in 1978, with the specific intention that it should be supplied by a fleet of five big river barges. By 1984 none of these craft was at work and the narrow, ancient streets, totally inadequate for the traffic, are now made hideous by an unceasing flow of enormous lorries. Had one set out to do so, it would have been difficult to select a more unsuitable site for an industry requiring continuous deliveries by heavy goods vehicle. Needless to say, the former rail connection was removed in 1964 by that shortsighted transport reformer Ernest Marples and his accomplice Dr. Beeching.

Leaving aside the question of what we are paying planning officials for if not to prevent the disastrous miss-siting of industry in relation to transport facilities, we may well wonder what benefits the so-called rationalisation of the milling industry has brought us. Perhaps the price of a loaf of bread is a fraction of a penny less than if mills were sited beside railways and canals and both home grown and imported grain was delivered by these means; or perhaps the product is sold for as much as the market will bear and the savings only benefit the huge milling combines. Whether reduced prices or increased profits, either must be set against the deterioration in the quality of life caused by the widespread use of artificially cheap road transport; the damage to roads, buildings, gas and water mains; the noise fumes and congestion; the appalling toll of road accidents in which heavy goods vehicles are involved. What person in his right mind can possibly argue that it is safe to allow a lump of metal weighing 38 tons to hurtle around the public road system at the present permitted speeds; anything so potentially dangerous should only be moved with the utmost caution and in such a manner that other road users are adequately protected. To the argument that this would raise industry's costs I am tempted to answer: so what! The Victorians, so admired by our present Government, did not quibble at the increased costs caused by the continual presure on the railways of that day to adopt adequate safety standards. Their legacy to us is a railway system as safe as it can possibly be made; why should we not take the same attitude to road haulage?

It is far from true, as Road Haulage interests are fond of telling us, that the country would grind to a halt without the heavy lorry. Economic historians have revealed that our economy was at its most efficient during the last war when only a tiny proportion of goods were carried by road, and that only in vehicles with small pay loads and restricted to low speeds. Even 25 years ago every town had its railway goods depot so that goods could be moved using short distance collection and delivery vehicles only and a good deal of traffic, including much general merchandise, was still being moved by water. The fact of the matter is that by allowing vehicles of enormous size to travel at unsafe speeds, with only token efforts made to control overloading, speeding and dangerous driving, and by subsidising the haulier's 'track' we have enabled road haulage to dominate Britain's transport to the detriment of our social well-being.

What is perhaps the most disturbing aspect of the lorry holocaust is the apparent apathy of the public. The most horrific accidents where people are mown down or incinerated alive as the result of the actions of some sleepy or reckless lorry driver produce no public outcry for something to be done. It is as if we were in thrall to some terrible god of ancient times who requires regular libations of human blood to appease him. Heavy lorries are often described as Juggernauts but those who died beneath the wheels of the Hindu god at least did so voluntarily.

Baddesley Basin turned out to be a small arm of the canal served by a mineral railway from the colliery which was some distance away. It was set amongst the fields with only a small pub and a couple of cottages nearby. There was the usual queue of waiting boats, those upwind of the basin flying brave pennants of newly washed clothes. Our turn for loading came the following day. We put *Columba* in the 'length', secured by a 'log', or half hundredweight weight, attached to a piece of rope, one end of which was fastened to the shore. The log hung down in the hold keeping us close alongside. A diminutive and highly polished National Coal Board steam engine, having previously removed the empty wagons, propelled a string of loaded ones into a siding on the edge of the wharf. When we were positioned alongside the wagons containing our coal, two men stood one on each side of the wagon door, and knocked up the catches. Down came the heavy door and a couple of tons of coal rushed out, the men holding their huge No. 12 shovels sideways against the flow so as to divert as much as possible of it into *Columba's* hold. Any that fell on the floor had to be scraped up afterwards. When the initial flow had ceased the wagon door was propped up with a stick so as to reduce spillage and the loaders climbed into the wagon and shovelled the remainder of the coal into our boat. Using the log we moved *Columba* backwards and forwards to get the correct trim. Clouds of coal dust which accompanied the operation found its way everywhere in spite of the cabin and engine hole doors being firmly closed.

John knew that the Birmingham & Fazeley Canal over which we were to travel was in bad condition so he wisely decided to take only 16 tons of coal. This was of the variety known as "beans" because that was the approximate size of each particle. With a full load of coal *Columba* would have been piled high but our small load was trimmed to lay neatly just below the gunwhales.

When we had completed loading and obtained our ticket, we pushed over to the other side of the basin to remove our coat of coal dust before departure. *Columba* had ridden high in the water when she was empty but now she floated level, her 18 inches of freeboard, or 'dry side', giving her hull a more purposeful appearance. Then, brasses shining and bright paint agleam she slipped quietly out of the basin, one of seven hundred narrow boats going about their unobtrusive daily business of transporting the nation's goods.

We locked down the remaining Atherstone locks and it took us about two hours to reach the village of Polesworth, a popular overnight stop for boats as it had a canalside mill converted into a cinema. This had unusual double seats in the back row known as the Polesworth 'Hold-me-tights'. Polesworth was also the home of Lees & Atkins boatyard which did a lot of repair work for the firm of Thos. Clayton who had a fleet of tankers. When they came off the dock at Polesworth they were in a handy position to go and load at the small Atherstone gasworks whence they transported tar to Oldbury. The main industry at Polesworth seemed to be the manufacture of earthenware pipes and there were piles of them stacked at the canalside works. John had enquired about carrying these by water but found that, although there were many waterside builders merchants, the size of individual consignments was small – about half a boat load by volume on average. There would have been a good deal more canal traffic in the 1950's

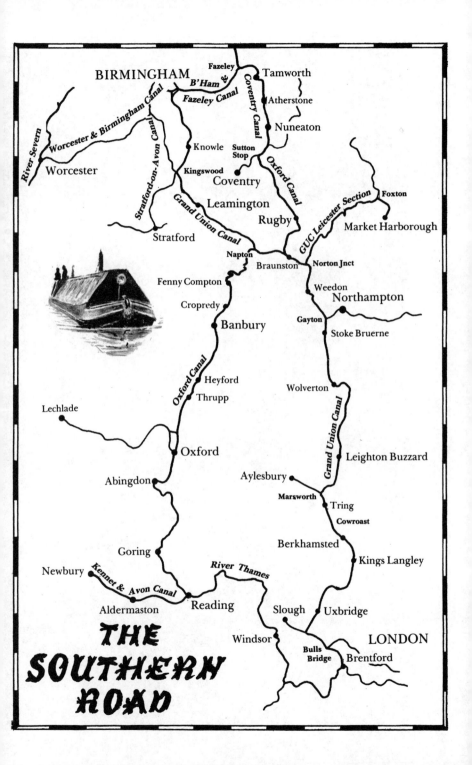

Dawn Convoy

if the facility for carrying part loads had existed but there was no organisation capable of consolidating such traffic.

Not far from Polesworth, behind small island in the canal, lay the loading chutes of Pooley Hall Colliery where several loaded Joey boats belonging to Element's and S. E. Barlow waited to be exchanged for empty boats; and we had only gone a short way further when we encountered one such vessel. A heavy booted urchin flashed a gleaming smile at us from a dusty face as he urged the horse forward while, at the helm, an old boatman struggled to counteract the wind which threatened to blow his unwieldy craft onto the mud. Behind the side-bridge over Alvecote Basin we glimpsed an empty pair of Barlow's. The surroundings were now a mixture of scattered houses and neglected looking fields as we passed through Amington, its colliery basin now disused, and approached the Tamworth suburb of Glascote. Here there were two boatyards, the first one being that of the 'Limited' which dealt mainly with Joey boats but on this occasion had the butty *Little Marvel* moored alongside. At this dock, after being winched ashore, boats were jacked up onto bogies which enabled them to travel on rails into a large shed where repairs could be carried out completely under cover. The other dock belonged to S. E. Barlow and opposite was his office and "The Anchor" pub. Both firms had a high standard of decoration but that of 'S.E.' was the more elaborate. Along the towpath opposite the dock lay a queue of Waterways boats which had come round empty from Birmingham and now awaited orders to load coal.

Below the two Glascote locks lay "The Park" public house which was a favoured overnight stop for Birmingham bound Joey boats. Opposite was Turners Asbestos Cement works whose products of sheets and pipes were again, we discovered, usually despatched in quantities too small for canal carriage. Rounding a very sharp turn, we crossed the River Tame on a brick aqueduct and came to Fazeley Junction. Here we had to make a ninety degree turn onto the Birmingham & Fazeley Canal. Like most canal junctions the clearance was extremely limited and I was told to jump ashore with a line which was attached to the fore-stud and to check her round. There was a bollard placed there for this purpose and as soon as the boat's stern had cleared the bridge which carried the towpath over the main line, I took a couple of turns on this letting the rope slip slightly so as not to break it, thus causing the fore-end to come round towards me assisted by the throttle and tiller. As soon as she was heading in the right direction I let go, coiled up the line and stepped nonchantly aboard, wishing that there had been some spectators to admire my newfound expertise.

It was getting dark and rain had begun to fall as we approached Curdworth Bottom Lock where we had to wait for a pair of lightly loaded Joshers, who were having some difficulty in the high wind, to work through, followed by another pair which we met above the lock. John explained that they were en route to Nottingham from Cadbury's factory at Bournville. Ascending two more locks we came to a lonely pub, whose faded sign proclaimed it to be the "Dog and Doublet", at Bodymoor Heath. Here we tied up in the company of the Joey boat *Saphire* bound for Birmingham, whose crew were spending the night aboard. After supper John retired to the pub. One of the crew of the *Saphire* was a young lad of about my own age called Joe and he invited me aboard into the cosy little cabin where the bitter east wind and driving rain were kept at bay by the fierce heat radiating from a small bottle stove on whose hob a kettle simmered. There were two seats, one lengthways and one across the cabin, on which the boatmen slept in their clothes, cushioned by a bundle of old jackets, or overcoats, which they carried with them. The fire could be kept alight all night by placing a banker on the stove, that is a piece of large coal with the grain running horizontally so that it took a long time to burn through. *Saphire* was loaded with D. S. nuts which were very suitable for our range, so I took the opportunity of topping up our coal supplies from her cargo.

Most of the older boatmen on the B&F Joey boats had formerly worked on long distance craft especially on the old FMC steamers, but the young local boys who usually worked with them had few opportunities for contact with long distance boats and my new friend was anxious to see our engine room and cabin. In return he insisted on taking me to the stable to see his horse. The dark stable was rather eerily lit by the flickering light of Joe's hurricane lamp which cast strange shadows on the wall. The horse stood quietly in his stall munching his feed and gratefully accepted a carrot. "Watch this." whispered Joe and I was rather disconcerted when he selected a long piece of straw and tickled the animal so as to induce an erection. "Horny bastard," laughed Joe, slapping the horse affectionately on the rump. "He's like me – doesn't get enough of it." This was my first introduction to the earthy humour of the canal. I was no prude, an English Grammar School education had seen to that, but I was, at first, surprised by the open manner in which the boatmen treated subjects which I was accustomed to hear sniggered over in some dark corner. Joe must have sensed my unease. "What's the matter," he grinned. "You've got one the same as him, haven't you?" I searched frantically for a suitable retort. "Yes, but mine isn't quite as big!" The reply seemed to please Joe who dug me painfully in the ribs and suggested that we go for a drink in the pub. I had never been in a pub before and had no idea how to order. "We're under age," I said, "they won't serve us will they?" "It's all right they don't worry about that here, it's too out of the way," was the confident reply. I was advised to order a pint of mild, half pints being too ladylike for rough, tough boatmen.

So isolated was the spot and so vile the weather that night, we found only John, the boatman off the *Saphire*, and the lock-keeper inside. They were all deep in conversation and only John seemed surprised to see us. We ordered our beer and were beckoned over to join the others. I sipped the dark liquid and found it thoroughly revolting. In fact I never got a taste for beer until I joined the Air Force. Nevertheless I manfully struggled through my first pint which, fortunately, was not very strong. The others were discussing our journey. The BCN is very complicated and there were hundreds of factories and wharves on its system. Our companions were able to give us precise directions. "Take the second turning at Salford Junction, carry on up the Eleven and the Thirteen until you come out on the Bottom Summit. They were referring to Aston and Farmer's Bridge locks. John said he knew where Sherborne St. was and we were told to take the first turn on the left after the entrance to Sherborne St. and to tie up just inside it on the towpath side. We were warned of the heavy early morning traffic in the Eleven and the Thirteen but advised that it would be reasonably quiet by the time we got there.

Now that there was sufficient light to see properly, I took stock of the *Saphire's* crew. The older boatman was attired in jacket and waistcoat over a striped collarless shirt with a red handkerchief at the neck. A wide leather belt, its buckle turned to the back, supported a pair of corduroy trousers held in by leather straps below the knee. Joe wore a heavy blue denim shirt (known to haberdashers as a railway shirt) open at the neck to display the patterned neck of a jersey worn in lieu of a vest. This was tucked into a disreputable pair of old trousers. Both wore boots heavily shod with iron. I mentally contrasted this with the dress I had so far observed on the younger long-distance boatmen, the most popular style appearing to be a checked lumberjack shirt with a pair of overall trousers, the outfit being completed by a battledress blouse. Nearly all the younger boatmen sported a beret, Joe's being worn on the back of his head, where it framed a carefully sculptured and Brylcreamed quiff of black hair.

Time was called and we had to leave the cosy bar for the cold, driving rain and the slippery gang plank, little more than a foot wide, which gave access to our boats. John went straight to bed, leaving Joe and I drinking a last cup of tea in *Columba's* cabin. I had let the bed down and made it before going ashore to the pub and Joe was lost in admiration of the spring mattress and clean sheets. "You've got a cushy little job here", he remarked. "We have to spend three nights a week on the bare boards. I think I'll stay here tonight and have a bit of comfort". This was said by way of a joke but I didn't want to bring the evening and the conversation to a close so I readily agreed. We finished our tea and had to brave the rain again to stand on the counter and relieve ourselves. "That'll bring the pound up a bit", said the irrepressible Joe, although the rain was so heavy that any further contribution to the water supply of the Birmingham & Fazeley Canal might be considered superfluous. Back in the warm cabin, we banked up the fire and turned in. We lay talking in the flickering firelight, Joe telling me about his family, their cramped back-to-back home in Nechells and his first job shovelling ashes at the Saltley locomotive sheds. He preferred working on the cut but was looking forward to his National Service and thought he might like to stay in the Army. Conversation soon lapsed though, as sleep has a habit of rapidly over-taking those who have worked all day in the open air, especially if they have finished the evening with a pint of Smith's Mild.

At some unearthly hour in the morning Joe's colleague hammered on the cabin side and he tumbled out to start the day's work. I also got up, put on the kettle and called John. We set off after *Saphire*, but with no chance of catching her as a horse drawn Joey boat could easily lose a motor on such a badly maintained cut. It was a damp morning, and a wild red sky appeared to eastwards as we locked up the rest of the Curdworth Flight, which was followed by three more locks at Minworth. In these uphill locks I had to bring the boat to rest without it hitting the cill by lifting a paddle on the command "Draw!" As the stern of the boat entered the lock John would step ashore to shut the huge, single leaf bottom gate as soon as the stern cleared it, for there was no room to spare. If the boat wasn't hard up against the cill then you couldn't close the gate. The surroundings were dreary in the extreme, especially when we got above Minworth Locks. For four miles the canal is lined by factories which would be well enough, but for the fact that most of them turn their backs on the water leaving a foot or two of rubbish strewn between them and the canal.

And so, at about 10 o'clock in the morning, we came to Salford Junction. Spencer Abbott's boatyard was flanked by Element's coal wharf while opposite two canals branched off, a toll office occupying the space between them. Beyond Salford bridge, noisy with many trams, I could see a wide straight canal disappearing into the distance and another wharf where many boats were moored. We swung round towards Aston and came to rest in the stop-place where the toll clerk came out to gauge us. Now the scene changed dramatically as we started to ascend the flight of locks at Aston known as the Eleven. The factories, and wharves which lined the canal on both sides all the way from Salford Bridge to our destination were built there with one purpose – to use Birmingham's water highway and many of them still did so. These ancient, grimy buildings reflected in the dark water held a strange fascination for me. And why not? Should we not find the monuments of our Industrial Revolution at least as interesting as those of past civilisations. It is sometimes difficult to explain why certain places fascinate and attract but, in the case of Birmingham's canalside core, I would identify two reasons. First the sense of enclosure, as for miles we followed a concealed lane of water completely cut off from the outside world; secondly, the element of mystery, for our route was punctuated by numerous basins and arms of the canal which disappeared into secret caverns of stygian gloom.

Other traffic was only moderate and consisted of horse drawn open boats loaded with coal, coke and rubbish, and Thos. Clayton 'black boats' which were short distance tankers; but there were numerous moored boats awaiting unloading or collection.

We entered the Farmers Bridge flight, the Thirteen, and the sense of confinement intensified. Now the canal ran in a narrow canyon of tall buildings and was roofed by wide roads and by the Snow Hill railway viaduct beneath which there is a lock. Only a narrow pier of slippery blue brick separated each lock and its adjoining side-pond. The latter were sinister pools of black water, exuding a creepy and perilous atmosphere as they disappeared into the gloom beneath low arches which supported some of the canalside works. Some of the locks in the Thirteen are very close together leaving barely passing room between them and, each time we met a horse boat, we had to vacate our lock and come to a stand in the short pound before the downhill boat could leave its lock and proceed.

Emerging from the top lock into comparatively spacious surroundings, we joined one of the two terminal branches of the original Birmingham Canal. Across the junction from us stood the tumbledown warehouses of the Crescent, the oldest canal buildings in Birmingham where the earliest waterborne merchandise cargoes were received and despatched. Night and day, for over 150 years, boats had sailed from the Crescent freighted with all the manifold variety of Birmingham's industrial ingenuity; but now the ancient buildings stood forlorn. No other place in Birmingham held such an atmosphere of the past; it was as if the ghosts of all who had worked here still lingered, loathe to leave the scene of their labours. They were to stand for over a decade before being demolished, for, to the eternal shame of the planners, these historic buildings were not included in the rather anachronistic redevelopment of the Farmers Bridge area in the 1970s.

We were now on the 453 ft level of the Bottom Summit and, having proceeded a few hundred yards further, we emerged onto the New Main Line of the BCN. In complete contrast to our previous surroundings the canal ran wide and straight all the way to Tipton, being provided with a towpath on each side, cutting miles from the original circuitous route which could still be seen in the form of loops which went off at intervals on each side of us. The first of these was the Oozells Street Loop up which we could see the piles of stacked metals and the collection of waiting boats which denoted Sherborne Street Wharf. About half a mile further on we came to the entrance to the Icknield Port Loop and on the wall of the adjoining factory a prominent sign proclaimed: Bellis and Morcom. I had completed my first trip.

CHAPTER THREE

JOURNEY TO THE NORTH

A s we had arrived on a Saturday, John decided to go home for the weekend, while I did some shopping, had my tea, and caught the bus into town to spend the evening at the pictures. The film that took my fancy was showing at a cinema in Northfield so I found my way to Navigation Street to catch a Bristol Road tram. In those days, long before the city was laid waste for the benefit of the motor car, it enjoyed a fast, efficient and cheap system of electric transport. Birmingham trams were renowned for their speed and had ample opportunity to make use of it on the long stretches of track laid out on central reservations and thus separated from other traffic. Much of the Bristol Road route was reserved in this fashion. To me, it was all very exciting. First the anticipation of the journey while queueing, then the scramble aboard and up the stairs hoping for a seat at the front. The rattle of the handbrake being released was simultaneous with the slight jerk as the driver moved the polished brass controller handle to the first notch and the ponderous car started to move, the wheels groaning on the sharp curve into John Bright Street as it rapidly accelerated. The top deck was warm and redolent of tobacco and damp clothing while outside the lights of a strange city passed by. When we left the street track for the reservation beyond Edgbaston Road the car was able to get up speed and it dipped and swayed like a ship at sea until the bite of the electro-magnetic track brake slowed us down to negotiate the narrow streets of Selly Oak. Another stretch of reserved track and we were at Northfield.

It was quite late when I got off the bus at Monument Road, but, although Ladywood was one of the rougher areas of the city, I felt no qualms about walking through the dark streets and I made my way back to the boat by side street and towpath happily munching a bag of chips. I delighted in my first experience of the BCN at night.

Down on the towpath all was quiet except for the occasional muted rumble from one of the factories whose lights were reflected in the dark waters. It was as if I had the world to myself. Before going to bed I stood on the coal box with a last cup of tea in my hand and the comforting warmth of the range by my legs, soaking up the atmosphere around me. The silent water and shadowy shapes of the moored boats seem to answer some deepfelt need, making me feel safe, untroubled and totally content. That the canal had such a profound effect could perhaps have been explained by my exposure to new experience at a very impressionable age; but the feeling was to remain with me over the years that I continued boating. L.T.C. Rolt has written of the sense of communion that he experienced one night when afloat alone on the Pontcysyllte aqueduct; here, in what an objective observer could only describe as surroundings of grimy brick and murky water, I felt that I was close to the very soul of the canal. The rural canals never excercised so strong an effect on me as did the BCN; wherever I was to trade something always seemed to call me back to Birmingham.

The sound of boat engines disturbed my Sunday breakfast and, walking the few yards down to the junction, I looked up the main line and saw two boats approaching in the distance. Soon they were forging past me, two of the single motors with 9 hp engines ('Pups', they were called) which I had heard about but had not so far encountered. Apart from these two boats nothing stirred, as the local traffic of the BCN rarely moved on Sundays.

As I had heard that there was still some traffic on the Worcester & Birmingham Canal I decided to walk to Worcester Bar Lock in the hope of seeing some boats, retracing our journey of the previous day as far as Farmers Bridge Junction. On the way I was able to take a closer look at the LMS railway basin at Monument Lane. There were many such basins on the BCN. A small arm was flanked on each side by sidings, the whole lot being covered by a canopy. Two wooden boats without cabins lay in the arm, one empty and one laden with rolls of newsprint, while several newsprint laden railway wagons stood alongside.

Not far from Farmers Bridge Junction the canal is crossed by Broad Street, a bridge so wide that it is often described as a tunnel. Under here there is a dark recess, a favourite resort of the local *filles de joie* and their customers. Beyond the bridge the canal opens out into a large basin which is divided by the famous Bar, the relic of a dispute between the two companies when the W & B was built. Originally all goods had to be transhipped from one boat to another over this Bar but, later, agreement was reached and a lock was built. This had four gates to allow for variations in water level. On the far side of the lock was a long range of stables facing the substantial warehouses of Worcester Wharf and a timber yard. The whole area was completely enclosed and secret and was deserted except for a solitary moored Ballinger horse boat. Searching round, I discovered an unobtrusive door which led to the outside world, access to the towpath in Birmingham being deliberately and sensibly restricted to a few places, and wandered through a maze of back streets in the general direction of Ladywood, getting thoroughly lost on the way.

The noise of hoofs clopping along the towpath aroused us in the early hours of Monday morning as the week's work commenced. The first empty Claytons were going past at about 3.30 am and the continual procession of these was joined at around 6.30 by rubbish boats of the Birmingham Corporation Salvage Department bound for Dudley Port. Then there was a lull until about eight, when the first black boats returned, by now deep laden with tar on their way to Oldbury, to be joined by an occasional long-distance boat to or from Sherborne St. Wharf. The coal trade was not much in evidence as the carriers, who were mostly based at Oldbury or Wolverhampton, would usually go out to the collieries early on Mondays, making their Birmingham deliveries on Tuesday mornings, but we did see a smartly painted tug belonging to Cresswell's on its way from Sandwell Colliery to the Kings Norton Paper Mills and, about noon, an Element's horse arrived with a boat for Canning's jam factory which was on the opposite side of the Loop to Bellis's.

Bellis's burnt a good deal of coal which was supplied by several different carriers from Cannock as well as from Warwickshire and, when we had arrived, there had been four loaded boats already moored. This particular part of the works (there was another section at nearby Ledsam St. where boats went through an arch in the wall to unload inside the factory) had two adjacent unloading places. At one, the coal was shovelled into barrows and wheeled over the towpath, while our berth was equipped with a gantry on which travelled an iron box which was lowered into the boat and filled with a shovel. The box had a grid on top to keep out any pieces of coal too large for the grate of that particular boiler. There was already a half-empty boat in the length and this had to be unloaded before us so as to be available for collection when the next loaded boat arrived. Thus it was after lunch when they started to unload *Columba*. The operation was prolonged, for the boats were regarded as a floating coal store, the coal being taken out only at the rate that the boiler consumed it. It was, in fact, well into Tuesday afternoon when the last of our cargo went out.

It was one of those mild, misty, winter afternoons so typical of the industrial Midlands, the sky being obscured not only by clouds but by the omnipresent haze of smoke. Somehow I always associate such a late winter afternoon, greying into dusk, with the BCN. We started up our engine, reversed out onto the Main Line, and set off towards Wolverhampton. As we proceeded at a steady pace, vista after fascinating vista was revealed, for the straight line of the Bottom Summit is punctuated by gentle curves each slowly revealing a new view. After passing the other end of the Icknield Port Loop we entered a cutting flanked by the Stour Valley line of the former L & NWR, emerging from it at Winson Green Junction. Here there was an island in the middle of the canal which left a mere boat's width of water on each side of it. On this island stood a neat brick toll house accessible by a narrow pivoted plank which the toll clerk, who lived in a canalside house, could pull across with a shaft and open again afterwards. Marooned in his tiny office with its cosy fire and racks of ledgers he would emerge to gauge the loaded boats. There were several such islands on the BCN, four of which had toll houses on them. Apparently only one side of most of these islands was now navigable, because, as a precaution against air raid damage, stop planks had been kept in place throughout the war, causing the unused sides to silt up.

We had to wait before we could pass through Winson Green Stop as a Guest Keen & Nettlefold boat from the Cape Arm to Hockley Railway Basin was in the process of being gauged. Every boat working on the BCN had to be weighed, that is, its draught empty and then with the addition of successive ton weights, was measured at a weighing station. The details were entered on a table and copies of all the tables were kept at each Toll Office. Using a graduated stick the toll clerk would read off the dry inches at four places on the boat, each marked by a plate on the gunwhale. The readings were then averaged and reference to the table would show the tonnage on board.

Beyond Winson Green we entered another factoryscape with many arms and basins and this continued as far as Smethwick Junction where the Old Main Line left us to climb three locks, each duplicated because of the heavy traffic, to the 473 ft. Wolverhampton Level. We went through Smethwick Weighing Stop, so called because there was once a Weighing Station there, and entered a much deeper cutting shortly passing beneath an aqueduct carrying the Engine Branch of the canal over our heads. The 473 ft. level crossed us again further on and, with the three locks at Spon Lane coming in on our right, we slid through Bromford Stop which had another island toll house. Because of its position at a particularly busy point, both sides of the stop-place could be used here.

It is about a mile from Bromford to Pudding Green Junction where the Wednesbury Old Canal goes off on the right and, in those days, Izons Turn on the left. There were many coal, rubbish and tar boats moored around this important industrial district with its gasworks, rolling mill and chemical factories but the scene was to change dramatically in a few minutes. Now we came out onto a high embankment, overlooking a vast area of wasteland stretching away into the distance towards the hills which flank the Black Country basin. This was once a coalmining and brickmaking area which was now worked out, leaving a landscape of hillocks and hollows covered with scrub. Mining subsidence had left reed fringed pools and there were occasional flooded marl pits. Such areas of wasteland were then common throughout the Black Country. Here in this heavily populated district were places where kids could go to let off steam. They could make as much noise as they liked, light fires, fish for newts and, in general, do just as they pleased without interference from grown ups. And when they were at school or in bed it was pleasant to stroll along the winding paths and muse over the remnants of former industrial activity, for, in those days, old buildings, railway lines and canal basins were not the subject of swift demolition, removal or infilling but were left to moulder for years becoming more and more romantic in their decrepitude.

There was a certain charm to such places which was totally destroyed when the bulldozers moved in and turned them into dreary housing and industrial estates and unimaginative 'public open spaces'. I see a direct connection between the loss of wasteland and the increase in vandalism. Although it existed, vandalism was mild in 1950 compared with today, consisting mainly in scrawling rude messages on the underside of bridges and throwing rubbish (which should have been collected by the Local Authority) in the canal. Schools, bus shelters and public transport escaped relatively unscathed. Of course, in those days, people that the media have now taught us to consider as figures of fun were then persons of undisputed authority; you did not argue with a railway guard, bus conductor or your schoolteacher. And this is how it should be for we are all born savages and have to be taught how to live in civilised society for our own benefit as well as that of others.

At Dudley Port Junction, from where we could see the mouth of Netherton Tunnel with the Old Main Line going over the top of it, we left the wastelands behind. The smoking chimneys of Tipton lay ahead and it was already dark when we locked up the Factory Three and tied up for the night next to a Stewarts & Lloyds tug and its train of coalboats.

The bustle of traffic on the move awoke us, and, with steaming cups of tea on the cabin top, we set off towards Wolverhampton. The canal was much deeper and, once through Coseley Tunnel and past Deepfields Junction it pursued a tortuous course. This was part of the original main line and boatmen knew it as the 'Hampton Pound'. The many blind turns and low-arched bridges were a test of navigational skill but, it being a Wednesday morning when all the tugs started off for the collieries at a very early hour, we were not in much danger of encountering one of these unwieldy trains. The canal runs through the middle of what was then the enormous iron and steel works of Stewarts & Lloyds at Bilston, now completely obliterated. There were dozens of iron open boats moored here, their sides characteristically pulled out of shape by heavy cargoes, and a slipway for repairing them. But Bilston, still known by its old name of Hickman's, used few boats by then, the principal canal traffic being furnace scale which was loaded into the boats in boxes and conveyed by tug to Smethwick or by horse boat to Wednesbury. It was the firm's tube works at Coombeswood which was a heavy user of boats and of this I shall have more to tell later.

We did not, in fact, encounter any boats on the move until we reached Wolverhampton. The LMS railway basin there was followed by the ex-FMC Albion Wharf, a most ancient and historic building dating back to the early days of the canal. Here there were a few boats tied up and we saw more at Broad Street basin. I remember being impressed by their extremely tall cratches, a style which was just going out of fashion. Between Broad St. and the Top Lock was a crowd of boats. A beautifully decorated Clayton horse boat was just emerging from the top lock, but this did not mean a good road for us as we found ourselves following an empty Waterways motor, which meant that we had to fill all the locks. Surprisingly we met no boats in 'Hampton locks and I must confess that I found the protracted descent rather tedious, more particularly as, having no bike on board, I had to walk the long pounds towards the bottom to get the locks ready. About three-quarters of the way down the flight there was an abrupt change of scene. Fields replaced factories without the more usual interval of housing estates or dreary modern industry. The bottom lock itself, only two miles from the centre of Wolverhampton, was a pleasant place with old brick bridges, stables and canal houses and here we turned sharp right onto the Staffordshire & Worcestershire Canal only to leave it, half a mile further on, for the Shropshire Union.

This junction, with its shallow stop-lock, toll house and stables was known to boatmen as Cut End, but its official name is Autherley Junction. Situated amid flat, marshy fields it conveyed a powerful impression that the traveller was about to set out on some particularly lonely and mysterious voyage, as was indeed the case for there is no canal with a more mysterious atmosphere than the Shropshire Union between Wolverhampton and Audlem, where it drops down into the Cheshire Plain. Unfrequented it certainly was, being then almost unknown except to those whose lives were connected with water transport.

A familiar feature of Cut End in those days was a sunken Clayton tied to the outside bank. The circumstances surrounding the sinking and abandonment of this boat are unknown to me but, on many a fine summer's evening, boatmen could be seen tied alongside smartening up their boats with a fresh black coat of tar.

Daylight was fading as we left Cut End and headed into the sunset. We were entranced by the moonlit lane of water through the dark coverts around Chillington and Deans Hall and by the twinkling lights of Brewood below us. After a couple of hours we came to Wheaton Aston and tied up by the old wharf below the lock. There used to be a particularly attractive little warehouse here, a gem of utilitarian architecture but I would be surprised if it has survived to delight the eyes of present day travellers.

In early 1950, the Shropshire Union was a very shallow canal. Its mud was of a particularly tenacious quality and empty boats were in danger of becoming embedded in it every time that they met a loaded vessel, so restricted was the channel. On the exposed embankments (known as 'valleys') the wind waited to seize the high fore-ends of empty boats and blow them ashore. Sometimes boats would be tied up for several days because they were windbound. We didn't escape an encounter with the mud followed by the usual exhausting struggle to get off. I would push the fore-end across to the other side of the cut using the massive 18 ft. long shaft while John would use a shorter shaft to try and push the stern free. This swinging of the bow from one side to the other might have to be repeated many times before the mud loosened its grip but, even then, there remained the difficulty of getting 'fan-hold', that is getting the propellor to grip the water so that we could accelerate enough to get steerage way. Quite often a boat would get off the mud only to be blown ashore again immediately. No wonder boatmen had a picturesque vocabulary; unrepeatable epithets would be slung from one end of the boat to the other as tempers frayed and arms felt like dropping off.

Traffic was sparse that day and we met only a couple of pairs of Claytons bound for Oldbury with oil from Ellesmere Port and a handful of Waterways boats. All these were close together, having evidently started up that morning from Norbury Junction. The boat that we had followed down 'Hampton locks on the previous day was loading at Cadbury's Knighton Wharf as we passed. On and on we went, deep narrow cuttings alternating with high 'valleys' which gave sweeping views over the Wrekin towards the Welsh border. After 17 miles without a lock we emerged from a particularly impressive cutting to descend the five locks at Tyrley. Now we were in lock country again until we cleared the bottom of Audlem.

It had been getting steadily colder as the day progressed and we found ice on the canal below Audlem locks which got thicker as we headed northwards. Near Nantwich we came across a solitary single motor, the *Holland*. Two children aged about twelve or thirteen came out of the tiny fore-cabin and volunteered the information that they were tied up because "our Dad's ill". A harassed looking woman poked her head out of the doorway and wished us good-day. The family looked poor and threadbare but the boat was scrupulously clean. The cabin did not even have a range but the primitive bottle stove shone with blacklead. For the first time I realised that life on the cut was not all bright paint and polished brass but could involve real poverty and hardship.

Snow began to fall and we were glad to tie up at Barbridge Junction and go below to enjoy our hot meal in *Columba's* cosy cabin.

Barbridge is a small canal settlement whose most notable feature in those days was a transhipment shed, the roof of which spanned the main line of the canal. Sadly, this unique building has since been demolished. The Shropshire Union Canal Co., which discontinued operations in 1921, conveyed small consignments as well as full boat loads and, as it had services to Manchester and Stoke-on-Trent as well as over its own extensive system, it was necessary to provide for transhipment between one boat and another. For this purpose, Barbridge occupied a strategic position. Cheese boats ran regularly between here and Manchester, much of their cargo originating elsewhere on the system and being transhipped here.

Ten more miles of rural canal brought us to Middlewich and to a complete change of scene. The fields and trees which had accompanied us all the way to the top of Wardle Lock were abruptly replaced by buildings and wharves. Hardly had we tied up at the canal maintenance yard, when we were passed by a horse-boat. This was the *Dee*, the last horse-boat to work for the Mersey, Weaver Company and also the last bottle boat, this being the name given to boats carrying chemicals in glass carboys. She had just come off the dock and was on her way down from Burslem to take up her regular weekly run between Weston Point and Manchester.

The orders for our load of salt had not yet come through, so, after getting some shopping aboard, we locked down three deep locks and skirted the large salt works of Henry Seddon & Son where the firm's six horse-boats were moored, their cabin sides aglow with the glory of crimson paint and decorative lettering. Just beyond Seddon's I was surprised when we came upon a solitary wide lock, on the side of which stood the "Big Lock Inn". Below here we entered a winding, tree-lined pound with very deep water, a complete contrast to the straight and mudbound Shropshire Union. Traffic was heavy and I stood fascinated as boat after boat appeared round the sharp bends and passed us at a brisk speed. The variety of liveries was astonishing; the black and yellow of the old established Anderton Company; the red, green and gold of the Mersey, Weaver and Ship Canal Carrying Co.; and the dark green of Potter & Son were all to be seen, as well as the colours of Joseph Rayner, John Walley and J & G Meakin. This was the morning traffic from Runcorn and Weston Point after which the Big Lock pound would become relatively quiet until the first boats from Manchester arrived later in the afternoon.

Around Lostock and Marston the scenery became more industrial with occasional salt and chemical works. The canal ran through several wide 'flashes' caused by subsidence which had resulted from brine pumping, and some of these had become used as graveyards for old boats. Subsidence had also affected the height of some of the bridge holes which meant that empty motor boats were obliged to dismantle their cratches.

After a couple of hours of this fast and exhilarating travelling we arrived at Anderton and tied up. The Trent & Mersey Canal runs close to, and fifty feet above, the River Weaver, to which it is connected by a vertical lift which transfers boats from one waterway to the other. Below us was spread out the panorama of the busy river and the vast ICI works of Winnington and Wallerscote. John intended doing a cargo for British Waterways if our salt order was delayed, but as it was Friday, he decided to tie up here, go home for the weekend and see what happened on Monday.

Left to my own devices, I set out to explore the nearby town of Northwich, finishing up, as usual, at the pictures. During the weekend I also discovered Barnton, said to be the largest village in England, and walked over the top of Barnton and Saltersford tunnels. The canal, clinging to the side of the hill, was wooded and pretty, in strong contrast to the busy scene below. When night fell, Anderton became a magic place with the shadowy black bulk of the Lift looming above the boat and the myriad lights of the steam and smoke shrouded works spread out below. The dissimilarity between our quiet moorings and the industrial scene beneath us never failed to affect me.

The arrangements for our salt contract were finalised early the following week, so we set off back to Middlewich where we were to load at the Cerebos works, about a mile north of the town. Cerebos had not used water carriage for many years as they had their own railway sidings, and it was a considerable boost to the morale of the canal community to obtain some traffic from them. Their wharf needed dredging but it had been arranged for a maintenance flat to be moored alongside and we lay outside this boat to load. The salt was carried aboard in one hundredweight sacks and we were surprised to see that it was supplied in a wet state. Loading stopped at midday and we were glad to be invited to use the excellent works canteen. Not long after our break we completed our load of a nominal 20 tons. John was of the opinion that we were at least a ton overweight which may have been due to an allowance for the salt being wet.

Now came the task of 'clothing-up'. The cratch had already been re-erected and the first job was to lay the top-planks on top of the stands and tie them down with the girder strings. The side-cloths, which, when the boat was empty, were rolled up tightly along the gunwhales and held in place by knee strings, were undone and the side strings, which were attached to one side of them, were thrown over the planks, threaded through eyelets in the other side and pulled tight, being secured by a special hitch. It was essential to get the side strings as taut as possible and secured firmly as sagging cloths were sneered at by the other boatmen.

The next step was to lift the top cloths on to the top planks. These were folded (or 'lapped-up') in such a way that they could first be unlapped along the planks and then dropped down to cover the side-cloths. This was easy, the awkward part of the job being to secure them with the top strings which were spliced to rings on the gunwhale on one side of the boat. The gunwhale on *Columba* was only about an inch wide outside the cloths. Someone had to edge their way along this, clinging frantically to the top planks and throwing the top-strings over them, and then make the equally perilous journey along the other side threading each string through its corresponding ring and throwing it back over the planks, where it was hauled tight and hitched. *Columba's* appearance was transformed by her sheath of shiny black tarpaulin which bore the slogan USE INLAND WATERWAYS in huge white letters. Finally we mopped off the boat and scrubbed the decorative white canvas belt and the sets of cotton line strings which adorned the cratch, also the ash strips around the counter. No soap was used as it would give a yellow tinge to the sparkling white ropes and woodwork.

Deep in the water, spotlessly clean and with brasswork shining, *Columba* looked a picture.

It was mid afternoon when we began the long climb out of the Cheshire Plain, lock after lock lifting us towards Harecastle Tunnel seventeen miles away. Nearly all these locks were duplicated to cope with the traffic of bygone years and even in 1950 there was still a substantial trade. We met so many boats coming down that it was rarely necessary for me to go ahead and get the locks ready. If the lock alongside the one we were using was full, drawing the connecting paddles (which enabled one lock to be used as a side-pond for the other) would automatically close the bottom gates of our lock. With plenty of water beneath us we made good progress, tying up when darkness fell as John was unacquainted with this particular canal.

Next morning our seemingly endless ascent continued until finally, we swung round a bend to find a line of moored boats and beyond them the black mouth of Harecastle Tunnel. I had enjoyed our climb up Cheshire Locks, its rural landscape and string of villages contrasting with occasional industry. Canal-side pubs and shops abounded and the very names of the villages were a delight; Malkins Bank, Hassall Green, Rode Heath, Church Lawton and Kidsgrove.

Boats were towed through Harecastle by an electric tug which ran to a set timetable. After a prolonged wait it emerged from the hill, sparks flashing from its overhead trolley pole, groaning as it dragged itself along on a chain which lay on the bottom of the cut. We attached our towrope to the boat in front of us, and, having removed the chimney and water cans from the cabin roof, crept into the low roofed cavern. Subsidence had so lowered the tunnel roof that it was impossible to steer and dangerous to raise a head above the level of the cabin top. Sitting in the lighted cabin we looked out every now and then, shining a torch to examine our strange surroundings and trying to make out the cross tunnels which formerly served mines under Harecastle hill.

After about an hour we came out into daylight and set off to traverse the Potteries. The entire summit of the canal from the tunnel to Etruria Top Lock was lined with factories and wharves and still showed evidence of a brisk trade. The larger wharves were divided up into separate sections for different customers and were covered with piles of raw materials for the pottery industry, mainly china clay. All the unloading was done by shovel and barrow; in the whole of the Five Towns there was not a single mechanical grab for unloading boats. Merchandise traffic was also in evidence and we saw cargoes of soda, flour, and borax being discharged. "Colonial Wharf", proclaimed the sign on the side of a warehouse at Mersey Weaver's headquarters at Longport, where tipper lorries were loading a Manchester bound boat with gravel. At Middleport, the large and well equipped boatyard of the Anderton Co. was noisy with the sound of caulking mallets and among several boats hauled up on the slipways we saw the livery of yet another carrier, John Green of Macclesfield. The smaller dock of the Mersey Weaver company was further on at the junction of the Burslem Arm. Huge slag heaps rose above us as we approached Shelton Bar, where the canal bisected the vast steel works, since razed to the ground, which extended almost to Etruria Junction and the locks leading down into Stoke.

Towards the bottom of these locks is Cockshute sidings, where two youths laboured with shovel and barrow to tranship a load of flints from railway wagon to boat. The large rail/canal interchange warehouse nearby was no longer in use. Below the bottom lock was the important Stoke Wharf of the Anderton Company; a basin opposite could be entered under a low bridge through which we glimpsed crates of ware being loaded into the familiar black and yellow boats moored by a colonnaded building. After we had passed the truncated remains of the Newcastle-under-Lyme Canal we entered an area of mining subsidence, several vessels belonging to the National Coal Board being in use to build up the banks to counteract its effects, until, beyond the colliery loading place at Sideway, we regained the open countryside.

So far we had enjoyed an ample depth of water and had many boats for company. Now the canal became shallower and, below Barlaston Lock, we entered the notorious Meaford Pound, where we ploughed through the mud so slowly as to seem almost at a standstill. After this, the four Meaford locks in their pretty setting were a welcome interlude, beyond which a further short pound brought us to the small canalside town of Stone with its boatyard, dry docks, wharves and brewery.

One thing that is fatal, on the canals, is to congratulate oneself on a trouble free trip before completing it. On the outskirts of Rugeley we found ourselves unable to get through a bridge-hole and no amount of reversing and taking a run at it had any effect. After we had been there a couple of hours a loaded Cowburn & Cowpar arrived. Pulling back out of the bridge to let him past, we watched as he floated through easily with engine out of gear, stopping on the other side to take our towrope and pull us through. This episode lent substance to our opinion that we were overloaded as our rescuer was also loaded with 20 tons; that is, 17 tons of carbon disulphide in tanks weighing 3 tons.

The face which Rugeley presents to the canal is neither ornamental nor interesting. There was, in those days, an evil smelling tannery and also a canalside slaughterhouse where we used to obtain our drinking water. Having been so long delayed, we were obliged to stop here to go shopping, a fact which I remember because I found an Army Surplus store and bought one of the battledress blouses which were then a favoured article of dress for the younger boatmen.

Not far from Rugeley lies Armitage, home of the Armitage Sanitary Pottery whose only use of the canal was to abstract water and return it so full of sediment that it formed a scour which brought us to a complete standstill for the second time that day. Eventually we succeeded in forcing a way through and were rewarded by a most pleasant and trouble free passage to Fradley Junction. Our friend with the Cowpar had been the only boat encountered since we had left the outskirts of Stoke, but, just after we had turned off in the direction of Coventry next morning, a pair of loaded Waterways boats passed across the junction behind us going towards Nottingham. Further on, at Huddlesford Junction, we met another pair of Waterways boats, this time on the Bournville to Nottingham run.

From the point of view of speed, progress was painful. Hour after hour *Columba* crept along, sometimes barely moving but never actually going aground. Slow though our journey might be, it was made agreeable by our surroundings; the peaceful lane of still water bounded by black hedgerows, its remoteness broken only by the occasional hamlet. To emerge into more frequented waters was like awakening from a dream. At Fazeley we had to hold back for a minute while a loaded horseboat negotiated the difficult turn, and we met several more boats before arriving at Polesworth where we tied up for the night.

Despite the fact that we were now retracing the route which we had followed when going north from Braunston, I was still so fascinated by the canal that I could not bear to be inside for a moment when we were going along; this reluctance to miss anything is something which remains very clearly in my mind, and was to last for several months.

Eventually we reached Braunston and turned off onto what were, to me, uncharted waters. Going up Napton Locks I was surprised to meet a pair of Claytons, having been unaware that tar boats traded on this canal. They were captained by Harold Clutton, whose son, Steve, was about my own age, and worked between Leamington gas works and the tar distillery at Banbury. We crossed the summit, lost in the Northampton Uplands, by a winding pound eleven miles long and made the descent to Banbury without meeting another boat. Here we found a pair of S. E. Barlow horse-boats tied up and were advised not to proceed any further as floods on the River Cherwell would prevent us negotiating the river crossing above Aynho Weir Lock.

It was to be several days before we could leave Banbury. The Barlows, worked by the Taylor family, were a 'one horse pair'; that is, the two boats were pulled by one horse. They were loaded with coal, one for Morrell's Brewery and the other for Oxford Co-op. They were almost the last horse-drawn boats on the Oxford Canal, being survived only by Joe Skinner and by two Clayton horse-boats, captained by Steve Dulson, which were transferred to this route from the Shropshire Union for a short while. I was indeed privileged to see these craft at work as the Taylors retired soon afterwards, living for a while in their two boats at Sutton Stop.

I was rather a shy youth and didn't get to know them very well while we were at Banbury, but I remember very well the piercing blue eyes and the exceedingly clear voice of old Mr. Taylor, who willingly gave me buckets of coal in return for pumping his boat. A boat called *Mabel* was also tied up at Banbury, her captain John Wilson, a Number One, having recently died.

When the floods had subsided at Aynho we set off towards Oxford. We were approaching a pair of boats which were tied up at Enslow when their Captain came back along the towpath and shouted to us. "You can't go down there", he yelled. "The river an' th' medders is all one!" He was referring to the section of the River Cherwell which the canal enters below the next lock and which was still in flood. Joined soon afterwards by the Taylors, we had to suffer a few more days of frustrating delay. Our new friend was Captain Dick Littlemore, who was bound for Wolvercote Paper Mill with coal. The floods had disrupted traffic to such an extent that the mill had had to send a lorry to Enslow to collect part of Dick's cargo.

Looking back it seems amazing that the trifling stream of Cherwell could have caused so much delay. After all, narrow boats worked on the Severn in all conditions of flood, having to make the approach to Gloucester Lock in very difficult and dangerous conditions as a matter of course. But back in 1950, I had only just started my boating career and knew nothing about working in 'running water'. Had I done so I might well have wondered whether the navigation of the flooded Cherwell, impossible as it was for a pair of boats, was really impracticable for a powerful single motor.

When we finally got going again we met another pair of loaded Claytons below Kidlington and passed them none too easily in the muddy channel. At Wolvercote Junction I was sent up to the signalbox to ask the signalman to ring Oxford and tell them that we should want the railway swing-bridge over the Sheepwash Channel, connecting the Oxford Canal with the Thames, opened for us. As soon as I mentioned the name of my stepmother's father, who had been a District Inspector at Didcot, I was made welcome, and, having gingerly tiptoed over the highly polished floor, was given a seat by the fire and a cup of tea until the signalman should have time to telephone to

Oxford. Meanwhile I enjoyed the atmosphere of the box with its long row of shining levers in their blackleaded frame, the ting of the block bells and the flicker of instrument needles. A long train of goods wagons slowly rumbled by outside, its engine simmering gently. What rewarding places to work were these old boxes compared to the soulless modern signalling centres where, deprived of any physical exercise, and unable to see the trains, a man is condemned to spend his working hours staring at moving lights on a diagram.

I would have liked to linger but duty called and I hastened to overtake *Columba* before she reached the next lift-up bridge. The canal had now become very shallow and we crept along, passing the once busy Heyfield Road Wharf (known to boatmen as Dolly's Hut). Beyond the Radiator Works, to which Joe Skinner carried coal for many years, we passed the Juxon Street and Co-op wharves, both still in use, and slid under an elegant little cast iron bridge into Isis Lock which admitted us to the Sheepwash Channel. Men were waiting to swing the railway bridge, and having passed through this, we entered the Thames.

The lock-keeper at Osney would not let us go beyond his lock as he considered that the water was too high; he was being unnecessarily cautious as the Thames in flood is a feeble river compared to, say, the Severn or the French river Doubs. We were allowed through on the following day and had a satisfyingly fast journey down to Reading, each lock-keeper phoning his colleague below so that we could run straight into all the locks.

At Reading we turned off into the Kennet, and this being the first cargo on that river for 25 years, were interviewed for the local paper while in Blakes Lock. Between Blakes and the next lock above, the river is spanned by a bridge the headroom of which had been lowered by the addition of girders inserted to strengthen it. The only way for boats to squeeze underneath was to have the weir sluices opened at Blakes Lock so as to lower the water level. This having been arranged we proceeded, but on arrival at the offending bridge, which is quite narrow, found the current to be so strong that we could make no headway. Engine flat out we were just able to stem the stream.

Just below the bridge was an old wharf belonging to Simmonds Brewery. There was a terrifying lurch as we dropped over against it and our starboard gunwhale dipped under water. I was clinging on to the cabin cant rail and thought my end had come. There would have been little hope of survival in those fast running waters, with no towpath and with buildings rising sheer from the narrow channel. *Columba*, however, righted herself immediately and we got a rope on to one of the piles and made fast. John gently eased the throttle but to our dismay the pile began to pull away from the bank. He hastily opened up the engine just in time to prevent the whole shaky edifice collapsing and avoid our being buried under a pile of beer barrels.

The situation was frightening. We could neither go forward nor tie up and had to remain where we were with the engine running flat out. The consequences had the engine failed did not bear contemplation as we had no anchor. Eventually the lock-keeper at County Lock, just above us, became aware of our plight and closed his sluices thus reducing the current. Inch by inch we crept under the bridge, uttering horrible maledictions on the Docks & Inland Waterways Executive and Reading Corporation. Once out of the narrow bridge hole our speed improved and we were soon safely in County Lock. It had been a dangerous and terrifying experience and one which I should not care to repeat.

At County Lock we were met by John Gould with his motor boat *Colin*, one of a pair of boats he had bought from Harvey-Taylor with the intention of setting up as a canal carrier at Newbury. We reduced our load by transhipping three tons into *Colin* and set off up the Kennet, which, now that its channel was no longer constricted and the sluices had been shut behind us, was a much more well behaved river. It took us three days to make the seventeen mile journey to Newbury. We did not have a great deal of trouble with the locks but there were several recalcitrant swing-bridges. The main difficulty was the scours which the river had formed across the head of each of the upper lock cuttings, a common problem on canalised rivers but made worse here by the absence of traffic and lack of maintenance. *Colin* struggled to snatch *Columba* over these scours; instead of using our heavy towrope, or snubber, the two captains decided to use a 6lb cotton line. As I had to be on the fore-deck to handle it, I spent much of the voyage in danger of being decapitated should it break under the immense strain. To say I was relieved to see Newbury would have been an understatement.

After some trouble in getting through Newbury Lock, (we had to throw hay into the chamber to stop up the leaks in the bottom gates) we moored up at West Mills. The salt was to be delivered to the premises of the Newbury laundry (it was used for softening the water) on a small lorry owned by John Gould's sister, Barbara; the heavy bags had to be manhandled out of the hold, on to the shore, and up on the lorry. Unloading took some time; when it was completed we locked down below Newbury Lock ready to start our return journey in the morning. That evening, I had a visit from a young lad called Bob Pettifer who worked at the Laundry and had heard about the boat. He and I had a long chat about working on the canals and he seemed interested in joining us. When John returned to the boat Bob was immediately recruited and it was arranged for him to join us at Braunston.

Some days later, we were crossing the Oxford Canal summit level with John at the helm when he ran *Columba* up on a submerged pile on a sharp bend known as Cabbage Turn. No amount of struggling with shaft and line would get us off so we had to settle down to wait for a passing boat to assist us. Traffic being so infrequent, it was not surprising that no boat appeared that day, although there were several false alarms caused by the engines of farm tractors whose sound carried a long way in such quiet and lonely places. We were miles from anywhere and there was not a soul to be seen.

The next day was the one on which we had arranged to meet Bob at Braunston so John had to set off across country to Fenny Compton Station to intercept his train. While he was gone an empty horse-boat appeared from the direction of Banbury. It was my first encounter with the legendary Joe Skinner, who must have unloaded at Wolvercote as we had not seen his boat on our journey up from Oxford. His wife, Rose, ran forward and cast off the towline which he coiled up and threw to me. When it was attached to our boat he urged his mule forward and pulled us free, resuming his journey with a cheerful wave and the words "You're welcome" in answer to my expressions of thanks.

It was late when John and Bob finally found their way back to *Columba* and we made no further move that night lest we come to grief on another of the Oxford's fearsome turns; but next day we were on our way early and by 11 am were tying in the arm at Braunston Dock.

Sunset on the 'North Stafford'

CHAPTER FOUR

"DOWN SHROPSHIRE"

·

B ecause of crew difficulties, John Knill had been working *Columba* as a single motor for some time before I had joined him. Now we were to re-commission his butty *Uranus*, which had been left at Braunston, and would henceforth work a pair of boats. Although I had now been boating about two months I had not yet had much opportunity to practice steering into locks or along the more difficult stretches of canal. Susan Woolfitt, in "Idle Women", gives an excellent and detailed description of the techniques of working a pair of boats on the Grand Union Canal, but this was to be of little use on the northern canals. Bob and I were therefore plunged in at the deep end and had to learn as we went along. As John had not, himself, worked a pair of boats "down the north' our methods were not always, it turned out, those of the indigenous boatmen.

When empty, a butty is towed up close to the motor and secured by cross-straps which lead from the butty's fore stud, one on each side of her stem post, to the dollies on the motor's stern, or, in *Columba's* case, a dolly on one side and a hook on the other. We soon discovered that on *Uranus*, as on all small Woolwich boats, the stempost does not project far enough above the deck and both cross-straps would some-times slip over to one side of the stempost. letting the butty's fore-end swing about. With the boats secured like this the butty does not have to be steered except to keep the stern clear of bridgeholes, other boats and the bank on sharp bends. This makes for a very relaxed atmos-phere when working an empty pair of boats three-handed. Except when working locks only one person needs to be steering most of the time; and there is a constant to-ing and fro-ing between the boats for meals, conversation, and cups of tea. Scrambling round *Uranus's* cratch in order to get onto her fore deck and thus onto the motor was a hazardous undertaking as the amount of gunwhale outside the cloths was even narrower than that along the rest of the boat.

The sensation of going along the canal on a butty was quite different from that on a motor. Gone was the noise, smell and vibration of the engine as the countryside slid past to the chuckle of water round the stern. When we got to a narrow lock the butty was cast off. Her steerer would give her a sheer towards the bank, run forward along the planks and jump ashore with a cotton-line which was attached to the mast. To check the boat, a bight of the line would be flicked over the fore stud and a turn taken on a bollard. Usually an empty butty was not steered but would be allowed to find her own way down the short pounds between locks. One of the crew would steer the motor, another would bowhaul the butty, giving bow or stern a shove away from the bank if necessary to straighten her up for the lock. The remaining crew member would be running around preparing the locks. With experienced crews, the motor steerer would start the locks filling behind him and, by the time the bowhauler got to the top gate on the end of his 70 ft line, he had ample time to push it open and draw a bit of paddle to help pull the butty in, but such time saving methods were unknown in the John Knill Navy and were in any case not for the inexperienced. It was a long time before I became aware of, and longer still before I mastered, the techniques which will be described in more detail later on in this book.

Although it was a regular practice, John did not fancy going through Harecastle Tunnel with his empty boats so it was decided to detour via the northern part of the Staffs & Worcs Canal between Haywood Junction and the Shropshire Union at Autherley. I was delighted to be able to explore a new stretch of canal, especially one which was so rarely used. *Columba's* engine had been playing up from time to time and it continued to do so as we worked our way up the Gailey Cut until we were finally forced to tie up at Penkridge. I forget exactly what the trouble was but it involved me being despatched by train to Wolverhampton with a bit of the engine. I had some time to wait for my train back, which was at about 8.30 in the evening, so I found my way to the Top Lock to have a look at the boats.

Two boys, a little younger than myself, were standing on the ramp which leads down from the road to the towpath. I joined them and, with a gesture towards the half-dozen boats tied up below us in the darkness, said "How would you like to work on one of those?" I was surprised to find that one of my new acquaintances had done some boating in the form of 'hobbling', in other words assisting boats up or down Wolverhampton locks. I listened, fascinated, as he discoursed on the composition of the British Waterways North Western Division fleet, learning, for instance, that most of the boats were iron built, except for three wooden butties and three pup motors. He also described the principal traffics; aluminium from Manchester, copper and spelter from Weston Point, all for Birmingham; sugar to Albion Wharf and flour to Broad Street and Bloxwich. The main downhill traffic was tubes from Coombeswood.

I discovered that my informant's name was Jim Beady and we were to become close friends during the time we were on the cut. After some time as a drayman and on the Nechells Power Station Joey boats, Jim was later to become a British Waterways captain. As the time for my train drew near, we tore ourselves away from the cut and Jim and his mate came to see me off.

Columba and *Uranus* remained at Penkridge for several days, much of which time Bob and I spent trying to scrape up an aquaintance with the village girls. I had thought the Gailey Cut to be devoid of traffic, but one very foggy morning I was awakened by the rattle of paddles at the lock and heard the unmistakeable "tonk-tonk-tonk" of an approaching Bolinder. Soon the long, low shape of a boat appeared; appropriately enough it was the *Gailey*, captained by Dave Wilson of Kidderminster, a 9hp BW motor loaded with firebricks from Brierley Hill to Burslem.

The remainder of our northward journey was accomplished without particular incident. There were no orders for us when we arrived at Anderton and we were to remain there for many days. The British Waterways trade seemed to be at a standstill and we were told that this was because of the approaching budget. Whether it was really true that all BW's customers had held off ordering goods until they knew what the Chancellor had in store for us I don't know.

Whatever the reason, there we were lying idle. One day a BW pair came up the Lift, the butty only half loaded. The captain told us that he had been to Manchester, Runcorn and Weston and had picked up all the remaining cargo at those places without being able to make up a full load. The Potteries trade seemed unaffected and the variety of this traffic did much to lighten the boredom of our enforced idleness. It should be mentioned that Bob and I were fortunate in that we were being paid a weekly wage; the normal practice was for mates to be paid trip money only.

Almost every morning we would awake to find a handful of

Knobsticks, piled high with crates and casks of pottery ware, waiting to go down the Lift when it opened at 8 am. The next traffic would be the boats which had started up from Middlewich that morning, some of them empty, having discharged coal at Seddon's, but the Mersey, Weaver boats were loaded with gravel chippings for Trafford Park. The morning trade from Weston and Runcorn would appear from about 10 am onwards with a variety of cargoes such as china clay, china stone, flints and felspar. Around 1 pm we would see the first traffic from Manchester, consisting mainly of flour-laden Mersey, Weavers and Coventry bound Cowpars.

Much in evidence were the beautifully painted craft of Henry Seddons, two boats being hauled by one horse, each loaded with 25 tons of salt. They would go down the Lift and tranship their cargoes to the steam flat *Weaver Belle* and her dumb barge *Gowanburn*. Occasionally a big, clumsy looking 'Runcorn' boat belonging to Ingram Thompsons would put in an appearance with a load of rock salt.

Most of the Anderton Company's boats bore the legend "Bridgewater Navigation Route" on their cabin sides, which gave cause for some interesting reflections. The original water route from Liverpool to the Potteries was via the River Weaver to Winsford and thence by road. The completion of the through Bridgewater/Trent & Mersey Canal route in 1777 caused virtually all the Potteries traffic to leave the old route. The Weaver and its carriers fought back by transhipping between the Weaver and the T&M at Anderton and prominent in this trade by the 1830's was the Anderton Co., which abstracted so much trade from the Bridgewater route that the Duke's Trustees had to take it over and operate it as a carrying subsidiary. The company became independent again in 1876 but continued to use the Bridgewater Route, on which they were the main carriers between Liverpool and the Potteries.

In 1949 the transhipment facilities at Preston Brook were closed and the Anderton Co. diverted its crate traffic via Weston Point and the Anderton Lift. From that date onwards, the Anderton Co., although it still had some trade from Runcorn and Manchester, was more in evidence on the Weaver; while the Mersey, Weaver Company, which had, from the 1890's, been the main user of the Weaver Route to the Potteries, became, by virtue of its large gravel and flour contracts to and from Manchester, the principal Potteries carrier on the Bridgewater Canal. After the closure of Preston Brook the "Bridgewater Navigation Route" slogan, carried for so many years, was left off the

Anderton Co. boats when they were repainted.

At last a trickle of empty boats started to arrive from Wolverhampton and there was a general feeling that we were about to start work again. Orders finally materialised one afternoon in early April, boats being required at both Manchester and Weston Point. Blowlamps flared into life all around us, but with our cold starting engine we had only to turn the handle and we were away, with instructions to load aluminium from a ship in Manchester Docks.

How pleasant it was to be on the move again! First of all there were the tunnels of Barnton and Saltersford to go through. Too narrow for boats to pass one another inside, they were operated to a set timetable which regulated the hours of admission at each end. Once clear of the tunnels I made a pot of tea and Bob took a mug up to John on the motor. Seated comfortably in the butty's hatches, with the tiller only needing occasional attention, I gave myself up to total enjoyment as we sailed along a canal cut into the hillside, high above the Weaver and with wide views over the Vale Royal.

As we emerged from another tunnel the scene changed as we threaded our way past a line of warehouses and transhipment sheds, the once busy centre of Preston Brook, where, ever since the Duke's Cut and the Grand Trunk were first joined, narrow boats had exchanged their cargoes with Liverpool flats. Like the Crescent in Birmingham it was an atmospheric place; what scenes of activity had these timeworn buildings looked down upon? It was easy to imagine the rumble of steam cranes as cargo was swung out of the holds and see in the mind's eye the boats jostling for position beneath the hoists. On that April day Preston Brook lay forlorn, its cranes and buildings disused but still intact. Now, like the Crescent, it has almost completely vanished and we are the poorer for our failure to preserve this historic and fascinating site.

At Preston Brook we joined the Bridgewater Canal running wide and deep the twenty miles to Manchester. We had not gone far when we met some strange looking craft, big, clumsy looking narrow boats working in pairs. They were fitted with timberheads at bow and stern and were of deep construction, loading to about 35 tons of coal. The motor boats had been converted in such a manner as to retain the original horse boat appearance of cabins, hatches and 'elum. The principal operators were Simpson, Davies and Jon. Horsfield. Both of these were old established firms, the former being recorded as having 64 craft registered at Runcorn in 1878. In that same year, Horsfields were operating 12 boats to Manchester, Leigh and the Potteries. In 1950, like the Anderton Co. and the Potteries carrier John Whalley, Horsfields was managed by a woman, the redoubtable Jane Horsfield.

Traffic was fairly light until the outskirts of Manchester began to close in. Warehouses, factories, power stations and gasworks loomed over us on both sides of the canal, which was now thronged with all sorts of craft. Crudely built narrowboats with their coal cargoes loaded in removable boxes, Mersey flats both dumb and motorised and 'Wiganers', distinctively decorated wide boats from the Leeds & Liverpool Canal, were all to be seen.

John had been told that loading might start that night, so, although it was dark when we reached the top of Hulme Locks, we started to lock down into the Irwell. There were three locks at Hulme in those days and the custom was to lock down the first two backwards and then wind in the basin above the bottom lock. The locks are underneath a railway viaduct and our toil with gates and paddles was accompanied by the rumble of trains; the shriek of whistles and the laboured pant of locomotive exhausts came to us through the night like the sounds of souls in torment. Finally we emerged into the uninviting waters of the Irwell which flows through Manchester in a sinister chasm of walls and buildings.

Tied abreast, we drifted slowly down this gloomy stream until we were confronted by a low swing-bridge. A shadowy figure emerged to open it in response to our siren and we slipped through into Manchester Docks.

We knew the name of our ship and that it was in No. 9 Dock, but none of us had any idea of the dock layout. To enter this vast expanse of water for the first time at night, with no idea where you are going, was a memorable experience. Eventually we found ourselves above the first of the big Ship Canal locks and knew we must turn round and retrace our steps. The docks were full of shipping but at last we discovered the right vessel and tied up alongside a flat, which itself was tied up outside the ship, waiting to load aluminium for Warrington.

We could have spared ourselves this nerve-racking introduction to Manchester Docks as loading did not start till morning. We were loaded overside using ship's gear and it wasn't long before *Columba* and *Uranus* were deep in the water with 42 tons of the silvery ingots, which were 'rucked' into their holds. This means that, instead of being landed in the hold onto dunnage so that the chain can be removed leaving the metal in neat stacks, it is landed straight onto the floor of the hold so that when the chain is unhooked and pulled out the 'lift' is pulled over into an untidy heap of ingots. On the Grand Union, metal was stowed in one ton stacks which were lifted straight out at destination: but in the North-west metals were always rucked. It was said that this was because a boat had once been sunk when its cargo of stacked spelter shifted but I suspect that the real reason was to make an excuse to have to re-stack the metal before unloading. 'Stacking money' was a useful addition to the boatmen's income. A boatload of aluminium, loaded in stacks takes up the entire hold and there is no possibility of it shifting.

Using side-cloths only, we sheeted up and set off for Birmingham, proceeding out of the docks and up Hulme Locks tied abreast, winding in the bottom pound and going stern first up the remaining two locks. This enabled us to avoid making a very awkward turn at the top to bring us round facing the Runcorn direction. At the top of Hulme we singled out. The 70 ft snubber, made of coconut fibre, was got out of the butty's deck, one end attached to the forestud and the other given to John on the motor who put the eye on the stern dolly and drew ahead slowly so as to take up the slack. When the snubber was fully extended he opened up the throttle. At *Uranus's* stern Bob put the big wooden tiller into its socket. As I climbed onto the cratch and walked back along the perilously high and narrow top planks I could see him struggling to keep the unwieldy craft on course.

The Bridgewater Canal is wide, deep and fairly straight and so it was the best possible place to learn to steer a loaded butty; an enjoyable task at first, after an hour or two it became very hard work especially when we got into the shallow waters of the Shroppie. It takes quite a while to become expert enough to keep the tiller movement to a minimum and for unaccustomed muscles to get used to the work.

From Manchester as far as Middlewich the canal is deep and progress correspondingly fast. By the time we entered the Big Lock Pound we had become sufficiently expert to navigate our unwieldy craft round the sharp turns where overhanging branches waited to sweep the cabin top clear of cans, mop and chimney. Fortunately we met no oncoming boats in awkward places.

The Croxton Aqueduct, just before you get to Middlewich, is only just wide enough for a boat and forms a convenient place in which to shorten up the snubber to a length of about 20 ft in readiness for working the Big Lock. After coiling the remainder of it on *Uranus's* deck I jumped ashore and went forward to prepare the lock. Letting go the towrope, John stopped *Columba* when she was halfway into the lock. As *Uranus* slid in alongside he caught the two sterns together and thus brought both boats to a stand.

Beyond the Big Lock the hard work began; fifty-nine narrow locks now stood between us and Birmingham. Our long cotton line was now brought out and attached to the mast and this was used to tow *Uranus* as far as the first of the three Middlewich narrow locks, being cast off the motor at a position calculated to let the butty float gently up to the bottom gates which, by then, would already be shut behind the motor. John then went ahead by himself, leaving Bob and I to bowhaul the butty through the locks, hard work indeed with a loaded boat going uphill, for the resistance in the narrow chamber kills any momentum painfully achieved pulling the boat up the intervening pound. Boating is mainly a question of knack rather than of brute strength but this is one occasion when a powerfully built person has the advantage.

Starting out of the lock was easier as we both could pull until it was time for the steerer to get aboard; for it was desirable to put the boat into each lock as straight as possible so as not to stop her completely through cross-winding.

Between the second and third locks at Middlewich there is a right angle bend, which requires the bow-hauler to slack the line and then flick the bight over the fore-stud so as to get the pull in the right direction. This was easier said than done for the inexperienced, what with the pile of coiled up snubber obstructing the infuriatingly small stud. Failure to succeed in this little operation meant that the boat would strike the wall of the opposite bank with a resounding thud and would, having thus lost all way, have to be painfully started again while unprintable imprecations were exchanged between the crew.

At the top of the three locks we rejoined our motor and were towed out on a short length of the snubber. Wardle Junction was the next obstacle and we would negotiate the very tight ninety degree turn by putting the motor smartly astern while steering the butty towards the outside of the canal in the hope that this would swing the motor's stern well out. Usually it worked but sometimes the result would be chaos as we struggled with shafts and lines to get round the junction and into Wardle Lock, all to the accompaniment of the usual bitter recriminations and colourful language as everyone sought to appor-tion the blame elsewhere. Jackson's Lock was not far away and the seven mile Minshull Pound which followed gave us a chance to recover our physical and mental equilibrium.

We were, in fact, making needlessly hard work for ourselves. Although it was timesaving to bowhaul in flights of locks there was no need to drag the boat by hand into the chambers of the more widely separated locks. The local boatmen used an extra long tow-rope (the word snubber seems to be more widely used on the southern canals) which would reach from the butty's fore-end the full length of the lock and on to the stern of the motor. The motor steerer would step ashore with his end as he entered a lock, and, while the lock was filling, would pull the end of the rope up to the top gate. As he went out of the lock he would start the gate shutting behind him, pick up the rope and get aboard, thus being in a position not only to pull the butty into the lock but to carry on towing up the next pound as soon as the lock had refilled. Some boatmen would even use this method up the flights of locks at Adderley and Drayton, but, as the locks there were closer together, it was really quicker to bowhaul.

However, this method remained unknown to us and we continued to struggle with work that an extra 30ft spliced on to our tow-rope would have let the motor do for us.

Two more locks brought us to Barbridge and another awkward junction. The Middlewich Branch is fairly straight but from Barbridge as far as Nantwich we were travelling over the former Chester Canal which twisted and turned to follow the contours. The mud on the turns was very bad and made steering difficult. At Nantwich we joined the old Birmingham & Liverpool Junction Canal which strikes straight across country using deep cuttings and high embankments on occasion. There are two locks together at Hack Green, where the lock-keeper's large vegetable garden was useful for replenishing our stores, followed by a three mile run to the bottom of Audlem. Here, Bob and I were set to bowhauling *Uranus* up the fifteen locks which occupy the mile of canal to Cox's Bank. This laborious, proceeding was quite unnecessary as a horse could be hired for 5 shillings to work a butty through this flight. I am glad to say that we availed ourselves of this facility on future occasions.

At Cox's Bank, lost in its shallow tree-lined cutting, a tap outside the lock-keepers house was one of the only two places between Middlewich and Cut End where boatmen could replenish their water-cans. A mile long pound brought us to Adderley where bowhauling was resumed up the flight of 5 locks.

It is beyond Adderley that the Shropshire Union begins to acquire that rather creepy atmosphere which distinguished it in those days. What Rolt had to say about the eeriness of Betton Wood in his book "Narrow Boat" could equally well be applied to several places further on. Skirting Market Drayton where boats had to be tied up in the middle of the canal, we came to the entrancing cutting which hides the bottom lock of the Drayton (or Tyrley) Flight; and when we had bowhauled up these locks yet another cutting lay before us, the prelude to a 25 mile stretch of canal broken only by the single lock at Wheaton Aston. At the top of Drayton was the second watering point, a spring feeding a shallow basin into which we dipped our cans.

Having got "out of the locks" some boatmen would journey on far into the night on this long level; but there were not a few others whom nothing could persuade to work parts of this canal in the dark. The most disliked place was Grub Street, although there were several other places which made one feel uneasy.

Nothing noteworthy occurred to mark the rest of our journey to Cut End beyond which we were confronted by the backbreaking ladder of Wolverhampton Locks. John decided to work the motor up first and then take down one of the horses which were provided by B.W. to pull boats through the 21 locks. These horses were kept in a stable at Broad St. Wharf. Clayton's had their own horses which were stabled at Cut End.

The first problem was to get the nervous animal across the busy Wednesfield Road. Being boat horses they hated the traffic. I admired the way some of the teenage boat girls would get on the back of a horse and ride it down the locks at breakneck speed, including under the low-arched bridges where the animal could easily lose its footing on the slippery blue bricks or crush you against the wall, but I had no desire to emulate them. This was the first time I had ever handled a horse, and I had a healthy respect of them ever since a young playmate had had her offer of a handful of food rewarded by the forceful application of a hoof to her posterior. "He's kicked me up the arsehole!" she shrieked indignantly, introducing a previously un-known word to my childish vocabulary.

We soon got the hang of working the horse in locks, simple enough when the animal co-operates but awkward when he doesn't. The boat is towed with the same cotton line used for bowhauling, attached to the boat's mast. As you go in each lock, the horse must be stopped so that the line becomes slack enough to lift it over the bottom gate. It then pulls the boat into the chamber and stops again when the boat is near the top sill. The boat is checked by drawing a bit of paddle and tied up tightly to the gate so, as to prevent the helm being caught between the closing bottom gates. Life for the steerer became interesting because Wolverhampton Locks abound in awkward bends in the short pounds, making it difficult to put the boat into the lock without cross-winding.

Although traffic in 'Hampton Locks was no longer very heavy, there being about eighty boats working over the route, the strict BCN rules about wasting water and taking turns still applied. The maximum penalty for wasting water was £5, a substantial sum in those days, and I was in trouble on this trip because, on my way down to help bring up the butty, I drew off some full locks so that they would be ready for *Uranus*. I was sternly lectured by the lock-keeper but fortunately my plea of ignorance was accepted. The correct procedure was to refrain from emptying a full look until the paddles had been drawn at the lock below.

Notices were displayed listing the regulations for taking turn. For instance, the horse had to be 'pegged-to' (or tie engine running) and the tiller had to be inserted. The minimum crew required to man a boat was laid down and no boat was supposed to be bowhauled through the locks unless attended by six people. Apart from the company rules, the local custom was for one boatman to tell the one in front "I take turn to you."

All these rules and customs had fallen into disuse, partly because traffic was no longer heavy and partly because the authorities could do nothing about the shortage of labour and the resulting short handed working.

Assistance in the form of hobblers was available to short handed boats. Ernie 'Jumpabout' Nixon made this a full time occupation but others would do it in their spare time. They were often kids off other boats which were tied up waiting for orders. It was not always possible to find a hobbler but, if you did, the rate was usually 5 shillings to assist a boat through the locks. This would normally take under two hours although the time taken to go to the bottom lock to meet boats would have to be added. Some boatmen would only pay half this amount and would throw in a tale or two about the days when grown men used to fight for the privilege of earning this amount. A few would pay better, some as much as 10 shillings.

At the top of 'Hampton we returned our horse to his stable and paused to stock up the larder before setting off round the deep and winding pound to Tipton. A few hours before, we had been deep in the countryside; now we were steering through the heart of Black Country industry. It was this everchanging scene, which alternated field and factory, that made working on the cut so fascinating.

It was late when we arrived at the bottom of the Factory Locks at Tipton but we decided to carry on into Sherborne Street some three hours away. *Columba* had a headlamp and John hung the engine room inspection light on her stern so that Bob and I could see where we were going. But in any case most of the canals around Birmingham were never really dark, being lit by the light of street lamps and factories reflected from the sky. That night we had the Bottom Summit all to ourselves and I found this purposeful journeying through the sleeping heart of the industrial midlands strangely satisfying. Life held nothing better than to stand at the tiller, a warm fire at my feet and a mug of tea to hand, the engine throbbing contentedly as we glided along in the dark, occasionally disturbing a courting couple, oblivious to their surroundings, in the shadow of a bridge.

At Sherborne Street we surprised John by executing the manoeuvre of breasting up without a hitch and were soon tied up and in bed with the contented feeling of having completed our first trip with a pair of boats.

CHAPTER FIVE

SUMMER CARGOES

•

P oking my head out of the cabin next morning, I found that we were tied up alongside a busy wharf. There were piles of aluminium, spelter and copper from which a mobile crane was loading a lorry which still sported the name and livery of Fellows, Morton & Clayton. Another crane was busy relieving a boat of its load of metal. From a neighbouring boat came a tremendous clashing noise as the captain strove to reduce his jumble of ingots to neat stacks, ready to be unloaded. Flanking the wharf area was a warehouse several stories high with a canopy extending over the canal. A lot of boats were waiting and it became evident that we should not unload that day.

A leisurely breakfast was indicated, after which we started to stack our cargo. The awkward part was to clear enough apace for the first pile, after which the neat silvery heaps of metal grew space. This accomplished, we paid a flying visit to the nearest public baths and rounded off the day at the local flea-pit – with its choice of sixpenny or ninepenny seats – followed by fish and chips.

Emptied the next day, we set off back to Wolverhampton, where we called at Albion Wharf for oil, stores and orders. Soon we were fetching out a horse to take *Uranus* down the locks on our way back to the North.

If skill is defined as the co-ordination of hand and eye, it is not a commodity too much in demand for a lot of the routine work of boating. One exception is the task of steering a horseboat down Wolverhampton Locks. Where the pounds are short there is little time to line the boat up straight for the next lock and this is made worse by the sharp turns to be negotiated between some of the locks and by the sideways pull of the horse.

Bob was driving on this occasion. Once the boat was in the lock he would draw a bit of paddle to help shut the gate and then run down to fill the next lock. Having shut the top gate, I would draw the rest of the bottom paddles, then, when the lock was empty, open the bottom gates, put the line over them and shout "Gee-up!" The boat would be dragged out at speed as I jumped down onto the cabin top and put the tiller in. If the turn was an inside one it was necessary to steer away from the towpath, try to point the fore-end outside the next lock and then straighten up at the last minute. There were only seconds in which to do this.

Needless to say, lacking both experience and instruction, we all made a real mess of this job and poor old *Uranus* was subjected to some terrible cross-winding. To stop the boat, Bob would throw the bight of the line over the forestud and take a turn on the wooden stump on the lockside. The more usual way was to use a gate strap, that is, to check the boat on the strapping post projecting from the gate. This both stops the boat and closes the gate; but we were not allowed to do this as John considered it banged the boat's stern against the lockside. As soon as we were in the lock I would take out the tiller, stand it up in the doorway and get off to shut the gate.

When we got to the bottom lock there were no uphill butties waiting for a horse, so one of us had to walk the animal back to the top and then walk down again, a total of some four miles. Had we been equipped with a bicycle the boats could have carried on and been easily overtaken later.

There was no delay this trip at Anderton. John went to see the lift-keeper, received orders for Weston Point and within a few minutes the huge steel gates that retained the water in the Lift tank were raised and we crept cautiously beneath their slimey, dripping bulk into the chamber, securing the boats firmly fore and aft as the gate seals could easily be damaged by contact with a boat. The lift-keeper came down to lower the gates, which were only inches from our stern, then retired to his lofty cabin at the top of the Lift to lower us down. The fifty foot descent took about six minutes and soon we were out in the deep waters of the Weaver, going down the wide river, with its busy traffic of salt and chemical flats, at an exhilarating pace.

There were many boats moored at Weston Point when we arrived in the late afternoon and tied up. It was customary for boats to remain there for the rest of the day on which they had loaded and to proceed the next morning. There were several small ships, laden with pottery materials, in the dock as well as some flats which brought cargo over from Liverpool for transhipment into boats. Every now and then we could see a large vessel going along the Manchester Ship Canal from which we were separated by a wall and a lock.

Spelter was to be seen stacked on the quay but the scene was dominated by high wooden trestles under which were mountains of china clay and stone. Ships were unloaded by shovelling the cargo into big iron tubs which were lifted by crane and tipped into small wagons which ran along the tops of the trestles to dump their loads in heaps below. To load a canal boat the cargo was shovelled back into a tub which was up-ended over the boat's hold. No-one seems to have thought of using grabs which would have reduced costs enormously.

After work had finished for the day, the docks became the playground for the younger boat people whose games of tag and hide-and-seek would continue far into the evening among the jumble of cranes, sheds and heaps of cargo.

In the morning we loaded 44 tons of Australian zinc (spelter) for Birmingham and were soon on our way back to the Midlands.

The next few months were almost idyllic. Spring slowly ripened into summer, the canal bank was covered with a profusion of wild flowers and the hedges took on a delicate shade of green before donning their maytime mantle. Life on *Columba* and *Uranus* drifted into a pleasant routine disturbed only by the occasional mishap inseparable from boating. The daily ritual would begin with the shrilling alarm clock followed sooner or later by the appearance of a sleepy youth who would only take on some semblance of life when the first cups of tea had been made and distributed to the rest of the crew. The engine would be coaxed or cursed into life, and, as *Uranus* responded to the first gentle tug of the tow-rope, her steerer would pick up the big wooden tiller, dip the end of it into the canal to ensure a tight fit in the socket and savour the sensation as the heavy craft first responded to the helm.

The exigencies of Rationing permitting, the aroma of frying bacon would soon float temptingly out of the butty's cabin. Once her crew had eaten their breakfast, one of us would have to get off at a bridge-hole, run ahead to the next bridge, and relieve the motor steerer so he could come back for his meal. We always tried to arrange things so that the morning started with a reasonably long lock free stretch.

Washing up usually had to be done in canal water, scooped up from the canal with a handbowl, that is a tin bowl with a long handle. It is often referred to as a dipper, but handbowl is the correct term, at least on the Northern canals. Sweeping up the cabin and peeling potatoes followed while those at the tiller got rags and Brasso and polished such of the brasswork as was within reach.

Even in the long lock-free pounds (it took, for instance, about 7 hours to go from the top of Drayton to Wheaton Aston) time never seemed to drag, although only two of us at a time needed to be at work. We never seemed to feel the need to put our feet up for a nap or a read nor did the long days leave us feeling excessively tired. When it was time to tie up there was just a pleasant feeling of a job well done. We would have our evening meal, a last cup of tea and go to bed. It must, however, be admitted that all of us found it an effort to get up in the morning.

One job that was always done when we had tied up for the night was to mop off each boat from stem to stern. The boats would have been thoroughly cleaned after loading or unloading but the evening routine of mopping not only removed the day's dirt but also prevented the woodwork from drying out. If the seams opened up, the cabin roofs would leak when it rained. At the same time the ash strips around the hatches and counter would be scoured to a snowy whiteness.

Planning ahead is vital for successful boating and we were not quite as well organised in this respect as we might have been. There were few shops near the cut on the Shropshire Union and, unless a definite effort was made to calculate the stocks needed, a lot of time could be wasted through tying up to go shopping. Wolverhampton Locks closed each night and also early on Saturday afternoons and all day on Sunday. We were always getting caught on the wrong side of these locks and, on one occasion, spent the weekend with the motor at the bottom and the butty at the top. Since boats had to take turns for loading and unloading it was as well to consider whether there were any boats that might go by you or whom you could, yourself, overtake (or 'pip') while they were peacefully asleep.

Our next trip was again to Weston Point but this time we loaded sugar for Wolverhampton where we unloaded up the Sugar Hole at Albion Wharf. Albion Wharf was a very ancient establishment of antiquated appearance and layout. It was once the headquarters of the famous early carriers Shipton's and the street in which it is located is called Shipton Street. In the 1850's it became a depot of the Bridgewater Trustees, Thos Bantock being their agent (there is a Bantock

Park in Wolverhampton), before becoming the headquarters of Fellows, Morton & Clayton's Northern fleet. The Sugar Hole disappeared under a warehouse at right angles to the canal where the heavy sacks of sugar were hoisted up to the floor above. The entrance to the hole was low and, once the boats were empty, the cratches had to be dismantled before they could get out again.

Next time we went down we had a complete change of route beyond Barbridge, being ordered to Ellesmere Port where we loaded flour for Wolverhampton. From Barbridge to 'The Port' all the locks were wide enough to take two boats abreast, which made for easier working. The sacks of flour were dropped down a chute at the mill onto the floor of our holds and we then had the labour of stacking them neatly in order to get our full load on. At Wolverhampton, this cargo was unloaded at the former Shropshire Union Canal Co's wharf at Broad Street where the boats again disappeared into a gloomy cave to discharge. Short nooses of chain called 'nippers' were dropped over the top of each sack and pulled tight before being attached to the hook of the hoist and pulled up, two at a time, to the first floor where a heavy shutter banged closed behind each lift. On the ground floor was a real curiosity, an old wooden-jibbed crane which had been mechanised by attaching an electric motor to it. On this level were stored cases of soda and occasional cargoes of cheese and other foodstuffs.

With so many cargoes for Wolverhampton, not to mention the delays when the locks were closed, we were spending a lot of time there and I began to feel thoroughly at home. There were usually plenty of boats tied up between the tunnel and the top lock; in fact I have seen the cut here completely blocked from side to side with moored boats during a Bank Holiday. The other place where you could tie up, which was opposite Albion Wharf and known as the Mill Hole, was far less popular.

Between Broad Street and the tunnel the outside of the canal was occupied by the large expanse of Can Lane Wharf, which was a Public Wharf provided by the BCN and used by several coal merchants. The tunnel, which was not long but was quite dark, was a haunt of courting couples, prostitutes and their customers. Boatmen would recall one such lady who rejoiced in the name of 'Old Fourpenny-bit', this being the charge for her services. Ladies of the night would also take their customers down the locks where there was little chance of being disturbed after locking up time.

Jim Beady would often come and join me when we were tied up at 'Hampton and we would sometimes finish off an evening at the pictures in the boatmen's pub at the top lock, where, as at Bodymoor Heath, under-age drinking seemed to be taken as a matter of course. He it was, who, one dull Saturday afternoon, introduced me to the mysteries of the Bolinder engine.

In 1950, the Bolinder reigned almost unchallenged on the north western canals. British Waterways (NW), Thos. Clayton and the Anderton Co. were 100% Bolinder equipped and, of the large firms, only Mersey Weaver's had a few cold starting engines. When I mentioned my ignorance of how Bolinders worked, the other boat lads regarded me in amazement. "I thought everyone could drive a Bolinder!" exclaimed Jackie Lowe (whose father 'Barnton Tommy' worked a smart pair of single motors) once when I was admiring his deft handling of the controls of the *Ling*, at Wardle Lock.

This particular day we were hanging around with nothing much to do, when Jim suggested. "Harry Barry's in the basin. I'm going to ask him if I could start his engine." Harry, the most easy going of boatmen, readily assented and left Jim to get on with it. With the doors closed to keep out the draught, the only light in *Otter's* engine-hole was the blue flicker of methylated spirits under the blow-lamp. Three of us kids were crammed into the tiny room, like acolytes around an altar, with the object of our devotions mysterious and quiescent in our midst. Jim pumped vigorously, there was a harsh roar and the fierce flame was almost frightening in the dark, confined space. As the hot-bulb began to turn cherry-red his hands moved swiftly over the polished handles and levers. A metallic clunk denoted the withdrawal of the spring-loaded pin in the flywheel. Jim put his foot on it and kicked hard, sliding his foot off as the engine hit compression. Nothing happened. Jim kicked again. I was totally unprepared for the sudden onslaught of noise and vibration which took place as the engine 'caught' and ran at full revs for a moment before the controls could be adjusted and the unmistakeable, rhythmic beat, the very voice of the Midland canals, began.

I had known, rather vaguely, that this was how a Bolinder was started but could not have imagined the sheer intensity of the actual experience. All the ingredients of drama were there: darkness, flame, heat, noise and vibration. Jim wiped the sweat from his forehead and flicked the reverse lever backwards. I watched, fascinated, as the engine slowed down until, just as it was about to stop, the reverse pump came in and the flywheel changed its direction of rotation. From then on I was one of the select company who were known as "Bolinder mad".

The doors were flung open, daylight returned, and the magic moment was over. I was back in prosaic Broad Street Basin with Harry Barry asking us if we would like a cup of tea.

As I got to know a few friends in 'Hampton and visited their houses, I became aware that family life was ordered rather differently than in my native Home Counties. Black Country women seemed more subservient to their menfolk who appeared to be waited on hand, foot and finger, even to the extent of not having to clean their own shoes. On the boats, some of the women even referred to their husbands as "my master".

The Black Country language was something else I had to get accustomed to; and, as some of my friends claimed to have difficulty in understanding me, I also tried to speak it. However, I shall spare my readers from having to translate more than the occasional phrase.

Next time we arrived at Anderton we had orders to load wool for Stourport, which was transhipped from a flat below the Lift. Among the other boats with the same orders was a single motor captained by Tommy 'Shek' Shackleton. The Shackletons were a very old couple whose home town was Middlewich where they were reputed to own several houses. We used to reckon Tom had thrown all his tying-up ropes away as he would keep plodding on, promising his long-suffering wife "Just a little bit further." Also with us was the *Arabia*, worked by Ike Wilson of Kidderminster. The Wilson's had a very attractive teenage daughter called Mim, who slept in *Arabia's* tiny fore-cabin.

With our holds piled high with bales we only had a combined load of about 30 tons on *Columba* and *Uranus* which made bowhauling an easy task on this trip. The Stour Cut known officially as the Staffordshire & Worcestershire Canal, but also colloquially as the Kiddy Cut because it passed through Kidderminster, was a complete contrast to the Shropshire Union. Gone were the long straight lengths, the deep cuttings and high valleys. Instead we twisted and turned, following the valley of the River Stour. Much of the canal was tree-lined, giving rise to its reputation as the darkest cut in the Midlands. It appeared quite remote, but every now and then, we would pass an isolated iron works or rolling mill, some of them on sites which pre-dated the canal. The only regular traffic left on the Stour Cut by 1950 was railway boats. Those of the London Midland Region were ex Shropshire Union cabin boats; *Symbol*, *Saturn*, and *Antwerp*. They worked from

Wolverhampton to Boatage Depots at Kidderminster and Stourport and were very smart in their glossy black and white livery lined out with red. The stern end of the cabin was white with a scalloped pattern in a particularly attractive shade of pale blue. The Western Region boats were open vessels of iron construction, carrying steel between Stourbridge Railway Basin and Swindon Forge.

As well as being dark, the Stour Cut is noted for its awkward locks especially the staircase at Botterham and the strange construction at the Bratch, where the top gate of one lock is right up against the bottom gates of the next. Some of the other locks have bridge-holes immediately below their bottom gates causing the balance beams to be cranked because of the limited clearance. We were told of a tragic accident that had occurred when a young girl had been trapped between balance beam and bridge as a boat pushed the bottom gates open, and had been fatally injured.

The Stour Cut, with its combination of remote countryside and old industry could well lay claim to being among the most picturesque of Midland waterways. In May, with the steep slopes above the river a solid mass of bluebells, it was particularly beautiful.

At Kidderminster Lock, one of those little incidents occurred which led to scathing remarks from our Skipper. The butty's 'elum, a large and heavy construction, jumped out of its cups. To re-hang it, it was necessary to lift it bodily by means of the tiller and try to line up the two hooks on the 'elum with the cups on the stern of the boat. When you thought you had got this right you pulled the thing up about six inches and let it go. It usually took repeated attempts before success was achieved. In the middle of all the sweating and swearing, a youth appeared on the lockside and asked me where he could get a job on the cut. Overhearing him, John grumbled "I've a good mind to give him yours!"

These relatively trivial incidents of canal life – going aground, getting tangled up in overhanging trees, dropping a windlass in the water – never failed to fray the tempers of those concerned. Later, when I worked on the railway, I was struck by the way how nice everyone was to one another in the most trying and difficult situations. It was very different on The Cut.

We were not to unload in the basin at Stourport but had to lock out into the river and go down to the British Waterways depot at Nelson Wharf where we were soon relieved of our cargo. Back loading of cheese was on offer but John refused it as it was for Tyseley. The

BW boats loaded 17 tons apiece, *Arabia* travelling via Wolverhampton and Tommy Shek taking the shorter but little used route via Black Delph and Netherton Tunnel. How I would have loved to take this never to be repeated opportunity to penetrate the 'back of the map' as the boatmen described the Dudley and Stourbridge canals.

What we did was to go down the river to Worcester and spend Whitsun in Diglis Basin where there was a fitter whom John particularly favoured. *Columba's* National had been giving trouble again and I had had the embarrassing task of being sent up to a garage near Wombourn to borrow some tools with which to effect a repair.

Diglis Basin was a delight. John and Bob both went home leaving me to enjoy it for several days. There were wide views across the Severn to the Malvern Hills, and, although the Worcester & Birmingham Canal had lost ·much of its through traffic, some interesting activity was to be observed, much of it centred on Townsend's Flour Mill. The mill owned two river barges, *Sunrisen* and *River King*, which brought grain up from Avonmouth or Sharpness. They each had a capacity of about 90 tons. This was sometimes supplemented by grain brought up by some Charlie Ballinger horseboats, which were towed up the Severn by a BW tug. Having discharged, they might then load flour for Tipton, returning with a load of Cannock coal for the mill. Other Ballinger boats, both horse and motor, carried "England's Glory" matches from Gloucester to Birmingham returning with 'big' coal either for the lock-keeper's houses, (on the Severn each house had an allowance of 4 tons a year) or for the steam tugs and dredgers; or chocolate crumb from Frampton on the Gloucester & Sharpness Canal to Bournville.

Twice a week a tank barge used to arrive and tie up in Diglis Basin. Her crew would then take a horse-drawn tank narrow boat up to the gas works about a mile up the canal, load it with tar and return to pump it into their barge which took about three boat loads. The barge, sometimes accompanied by its attendant boat, would then depart for the tar distillery at Sandhurst near Gloucester.

When I got tired of the basin I could walk down the river a short way to Diglis Wharf and Oil Depot which was constantly busy with enormous estuarial barges and tankers.

There was a load of canned tomatoes for Birmingham on offer but John turned it down, partly because of the low rate and partly because of the need to bow-haul through the fifty-six locks in the first sixteen miles to Tardebigge. We didn't know that we could have had one of the BW horses which were stabled at Worcester and hired by the trip. He may well, also, have had some doubts as to how his crew would perform in the mile long tunnel at Kings Norton. So back we went to Anderton, retracing our steps up the Severn, the Stour Cut and "down Shropshire".

Going down Audlem this time, I had a nasty fright. I was driving the horse and, standing between the line and the lock-side, lost my balance. I grabbed at the only thing to hand which was the line and luckily the horse kept pulling, keeping the line tight and saving me from falling in the lock right in front of the oncoming boat.

"Dates for Fazeley Street" we were told by the lift-keeper and we tied up below the Lift to find that the flats had already arrived and several boats were loading. The dates were wrapped in a woven straw covering encased in sacking. Many of the casings were ripped, exposing the cargo. We sheeted up in the usual way, that is with the planks on top of the stands, giving ample room for our holds to become infested with flies. On *Uranus*, which, of course, had no intervening engine-hole, the smell was horrible. It was very hot weather.

Other boatmen, more crafty than us, had laid their planks on top of the cargo so that the cloths closely covered it, keeping down flies and smell.

To get to Fazeley Street we had to go down the Thirteen, turn right at the top of the Eleven and descend Ashted Locks, an extra nineteen locks, bowhauling through which aroused little enthusiasm. Time was when horses were provided but they had been removed about the time of Nationalisation.

The canal emerges from the bottom lock of Ashted into a tunnel after which there is a sharp turn from the BCN on to the Warwick & Birmingham Canal at Digbeth Junction, commonly known as Warwick Bar. Anyone missing the turn would end up in the premises of the Typhoo Tea Company in Digbeth Basin. Strangers have been known to do this!

The name Fazeley Street covered several wharves and warehouses between Digbeth and Bordesley Junction, the largest being New Fazeley Street (sometimes known as Warwick Wharf); but we were destined for the original FMC headquarters now belonging to HP Sauce. We tied up under a large, airy shed; the very place from which generations of fly-boats had arrived and departed, but now stacked with the raw materials of sauce making.

As was usually the case with HP Sauce traffic there was a prolonged delay before we were unloaded. Not only were individual shipments quite large, meaning that a lot of boats would arrive together, but there was also a shortage of storage space. When the huge amounts of HP Sauce ingredients moved by canal are considered, the mind boggles at the quantity of the resulting product ultimately consumed.

John had just bought two motor boats from the Flixborough Shipping Co, and was having them docked by Mersey, Weaver's at Burslem, so he whisked Bob up there for a couple of days leaving me to hold the fort. I was quite happy exploring the surrounding area and taking a few tram rides. There was plenty of traffic on the canal, both local craft and also BW boats from London which unloaded at Warwick Wharf, where, besides the large, modern warehouse, there was open storage for metal traffic.

While the dates were coming out of *"Uranus"* we found two rats in the hold which resulted in a frantic chase with sticks until they were cornered and killed. I often think of them as I shake the sticky, brown liquid over my bacon and eggs.

CHAPTER SIX

HAMPTON COURT AND MARKET HARBOROUGH

•

O rders for more salt had come through and for this trip it had been decided to use two motors, so we left *Uranus* at British Waterway's maintenance yard above Middlewich locks. Our new motor was named *Kenelm* and was very smart in her newly painted livery of blue and oak grain. John decided to put 23 tons on each motor, an unheard of load on the northern canals. Potteries boats loaded 20 tons per boat whether motor or butty, while Joshers going south of the Potteries would load 18 tons on a motor and 22 tons on the butty.

All went well on the long ascent of Cheshire Locks although I wasn't pleased at having to do all the bank work for both boats; in Harecastle Tunnel I could hear *Columba* occasionally scraping the bottom but we were spared the unpleasant experience of being stuck in those gloomy depths. When we started up our engines at Chatterley some problems manifested themselves on *Kenelm* so I was told to carry on by myself with *Columba* and tie up at Etruria Top Lock. It wasn't long before *Kenelm* was out of sight and I was on my own, the first time I had been in independant charge of a motor boat. We had delayed so long at Chatterley that it was dark by the time I got to Longport but seeing to steer was no problem and there was plenty of water. Or so I thought until *Columba* came to a dead halt at Shelton Bar, right in the middle of the steel works. I adopted the usual procedure of reversing and then approaching the scour very slowly in the hope of floating over out of gear. This didn't work so I had to resort to taking a run at it, and, after several attempts, managed to force a way through.

Safely moored up at Etruria, I was chatting to Mrs. Bunn, whose loaded pair of Potter's was tied up there, when her husband arrived out of the darkness on his bike. "Mester Knill says you'm to goo back to Maersy Weever's dock," he proclaimed. There was nothing for it but to wind my heavily laden boat and set off, not without some trepidation. Fortunately, I had driven a good channel through the scour at Shelton and *Columba* did no more than scrape the bottom. As I approached Burslem I saw a head appear above *Kenelm's* cabin slide and hoped whoever it was would be suitably impressed by my feat of single-handed boatmanship. John and Bob, however, were preoccupied with *Kenelm's* National which gave every promise of being even more troublesome than that in *Columba*.

After some engine adjustments we got away the following afternoon, diverted, down Stoke Locks, by the antics of two playful girls. Many of the Trent & Mersey locks have a little foot-bridge across the tail consisting of two cantilevered parts which leave a gap in the middle for the towline to go through. Girls would sometimes stand on the footbridge as a boat went underneath, with a foot each side of the gap, knowing full well·that the boatman could look up and get a brief but enticing glimpse up their skirts. In the early 1950's it was not unusual for the male inhabitants of the industrial midlands not to wear underclothes, such garments being regarded as sissy. Going down Stoke locks that day, I was able to make the interesting discovery that the female of the species sometimes went knickerless, a habit that I had been told about but had not previously believed.

The usual crawl along the Meaford Pound was even more painful than usual – we could hardly see ourselves moving most of the way. It was late when we got to Stone so we tied up and called it a day.

A pleasant surprise awaited us the next morning. The North Western Division of British Waterays had decided that something should be done about their mud-choked inheritance and had embarked on a massive dredging programme to be carried out by using dragline dredgers operating from the bank. These were much more effective than the usual steam dredger but, of course, could only be used where access to the bank was possible. Dredging was therefore rather patchy but large mileages were cleaned out in a very short time. We had not gone far below Stone when we encountered a dragline at work. As we passed him, the driver told us that every time a loaded boat came down it gave him another hour's work, an indication of how much mud a boat would push in front of it.

Kenelm's engine was still playing up, so, instead of one of us going ahead to get the locks ready, I was told to go ahead with *Columba* and wait at Haywood. The dragline had been working up from Haywood so I had a most exhilarating run as *Columba* sped down the Trent Valley with plenty of water under her. None of the locks were ready so I had to stop above each one and fill it, opening the top gate and climbing back aboard the boat to drive her in. The Trent & Mersey (Midlands boatmen sometimes called it the North Stafford because it had once belonged to the railway company of the same name) had very deep locks and, when the chamber was empty, I found it difficult to get the bottom gates open against the pressure of the boat, which, in accordance with our usual method, had been left ticking over in forward gear. I couldn't leave her out of gear and, having opened the bottom gates, jump down on the cabin top – it was much too great a drop – so I solved the problem by flushing her out of the chamber with a bit of top paddle. As soon as the fore-end came abreast of the bottom steps I was able to get aboard, walk along the top planks to the stern, and drive her out of the lock. There are other ways of dealing with this problem but I didn't know them at the time.

More delay occurred at Haywood while we tinkered with *Kenelm's* engine; few examples of its breed can have incurred more verbal abuse. So far were we behind on our schedule that we decided to work all night to catch up, as once below Colwich Lock, there were only the three locks at Fradley in an otherwise lock-free stretch of about 22 miles.

Excited by the prospect of having charge of *Columba* all night, I was again sent ahead and soon left *Kenelm* far behind. All went well until I came to Brindley's Bank where the propellor hit a rock on the outside of the difficult right-angle bend, breaking the shear-pin in the intermediate shaft coupling. I took up the cabin floor-boards and fitted a new shear-pin but had hardly gone a few yards in the dark when I broke another followed by yet a third. Fortunately we had a good supply of shear-pins and, as *Kenelm* was nowhere in sight, I was able to keep this incident a secret. Had our Skipper discovered it he would undoubtedly have been far from pleased, despite the fact that I had only been along this canal once before and couldn't be expected to know the bad places.

As built, all these ex Grand Union motor boats were not equipped with shear-pins and hitting a hard obstruction with the propellor would often result in fracturing the cast iron coupling; but *Columba* had done this on an earlier occasion and John had had shearpins fitted while we were at Diglis.

Congratulating myself on getting out of this bit of trouble, I boated on through the summer night; but not for long because I became fast in that same bridge-hole at Rugeley where we had experienced trouble

Heading South from Preston Brook

"Eagle", 'Down Shropshire'.

on the first salt run. No amount of backing and filling had any effect; after a while the dim shape of *Kenelm* appeared through the dark and there we had to stay until a phone call to BW brought us the assistance of a hand operated spoon dredger. This was a narrow boat fitted with a small crane from which hung the scoop, a perforated spoon on the end of a long handle which was pushed into the mud and then laboriously winched up, bringing up some two hundred weights or so of mud at a time, until we were able to float through the bridge. To add insult to injury, John subsequently received a bill from BW charging him for the use of the dredger on the grounds that we were overloaded.

Foreseeing more trouble at Armitage, John now came to the decision to lighten the boats by three tons apiece. We loaded the salt onto a lorry and arranged for it to be brought to us at Glascote for reloading. Even then our troubles were not over. Before we could shake off the unlikeable surroundings of Rugeley, more fiddling with the engines was necessary, this time requiring the use of a pair of 'footprints' a tool which we lacked. As usual I was selected for the embarrassing task of walking to the nearest garage and persuading the reluctant proprietor to lend us the tool.

After some groping in the engine's innards, triumphal cries were heard, the engine was started and I was sent back to the garage to return the tool. Hardly had we let go when the engine failed again and I was once again despatched to the garage to be greeted by sardonic remarks from the amused staff. Amid the miasmic stench of Rugeley's canalside slaughterhouse Bob and John returned to the task of delving in *Kenelm's* entrails, all the while encouraging the recalcitrant machinery with vile curses. Once again the engine was started. Once again we untied and started to proceed. Once again I returned the footprints to their owner and rejoined the boats only to find that they had again broken down. In spite of my suggestion that a visit to the garage would soothe the tempers of my mates, they insisted that I should go and borrow the wretched tool for the third time. And so, red-faced and sweating, I once again presented myself at the garage to beg for the loan of the hated footprints. This time the efforts of my companions met with more lasting success and I was able to deposit the tool with its owner for good. It was by now, rather late in the day and we had to make a non-stop run to Glascote in order to make our early morning rendezvous with the lorry, carrying on to Sutton's Stop that night.

For a couple of days we were free of engine trouble and were able to enjoy our boating and the beautiful June weather. Going up Hill-morton we caught up with Dick Littlemore's son, Charlie, with a pair of coal boats bound for Oxford, but he pulled ahead of us and was out of our way going up Napton. At Marston Doles we tied up in the company of Joe Skinner, Charlie having carried on, possible to Fenny Compton, three hours travelling away, or perhaps just a mile or two round the Eleven Mile. Boatmen often did this, knowing that they would feel the water moving when a boat started up from Marston Doles and thus have time to start their own engine and keep in front.

Joe was away at 4am on a perfect morning and we followed a couple of hours later. Napton Summit seemed more beautiful than ever as we swung this way and that, round bend after bend under a cloudless sky, with myself humming a little ditty called "Candy and Cake", which enjoyed a brief popularity at the time and the sound of which today brings back the memory of that halcyon summer day "up 'leven mile pound" with almost painful clarity.

More engine trouble occurred at Kings Sutton and John decided to send me by train to the British Waterways depot at Bulls Bridge for a replacement part. BW's large fleet of National engines was main-tained from there and, over the years, they had made so many of their own parts that it was said that they were more "Bulls Bridge Engines" than National engines. It was arranged that I should rejoin the boats at Heyford where the station is right by the cut.

An early mist was rising from the water meadows when the local train drew into Kings Sutton station. After changing trains at Oxford, Didcot and Reading I finally arrived at Hayes from where I walked to Bulls Bridge. It was here that I suffered one of those encounters with petty bureaucracy which were typical of the period.

In these days, when you can walk into a bank and find it full of customers, many of them teenagers, in working clothes, it may be hard to imagine how different things were in 1950. For a young workman to enter a bank where he did not have an account was to risk being treated with the utmost disdain by the counter staff. Minor clerks of all descriptions, including those in Post Offices, were often rude and unhelpful. On this occasion I was kept hanging around for an extremely long time before being attended to and I became very worried about missing the last connection back to Heyford. Explaining this to the clerk in the Waterway's office I asked if he would telephone for a taxi for me, a request that was refused so indignantly that I might have been asking for the Crown Jewels. With visions of spending the night on some railway junction, I grabbed the spare part and ran most of the way to Hayes station, boarding the train just as it was pulling out. I suppose it is natural to look back on the 1950s with nostalgia but there were certainly some aspects of life the disappearance of which nobody can regret.

To the best of my recollection, this episode saw the last of our engine trouble for the time being; but fate had one more blow in store for us before we arrived at Reading. Entering one of the lock-cuts on the Thames, Bob got firmly aground with *Kenelm*. Attempts to pull her off with a cotton line resulted in most of it becoming wrapped around her blades. This was one of the worse things that could happen on the cut. From time to time boats would pick up all sorts of things on their propellors – bits of rope, wire, old tyres – which could sometimes be dislodged by a quick 'chuck astern'. If this didn't work it was necessary to rake out the blades with a shaft, often a long and exasperating task. There were some occasions when no amount of pulling and prodding with the shaft would free the propellor and this proved to be one of them. We had to complete our trip tied abreast, powered only by *Columba*, and, on arrival at Reading, unload *Kenelm* stern first so as to raise her blades out of the water. Once the rope could be seen, it was then possible, though still difficult, to remove it.

Needless to say, the incident called forth the wrath of our Skipper, such an appalling trip being enough to try the patience of a saint, and I was glad that, for once, I had been responsible neither for the original grounding nor for the subsequent debacle.

A good deal of credit must be given to John Knill for introducing the Denyer Hoist to canal carrying. This was a small, petrol driven hoist which could be carried on the boat and enabled us to transfer bagged goods to lorry anywhere where we could come alongside. All that was needed was for the lorry to be fitted with a socket into which the hoist was fitted. John had arranged for a local coal merchant to equip one of his lorries with a socket in order to do our deliveries and unloading went on briskly. We had one boatload for Newbury which was forwarded from Reading by road, while the other contained various types of salt for several customers in Reading.

At that time, a good deal of top-soil from the Newbury area was sent to the outskirts of London for use in market gardening. Two boatloads of this comprised our next cargo, loaded at Reading for a nursery at Hampton Court. Bob went off on leave and John and I had a pleasant and uneventful trip down river. At Hampton Court we took some photos for a publicity blotter (no ball-point pens in those days). The photo showed me at the helm of *Kenelm* and the Blurb included the words "... safe in the hands of one skilled boat Captain......" I was very proud of this, after all who was to know that I was neither skilled nor a Captain, and kept one of these blotters for years. If any survive today they would be collector's items.

The cargo was discharged by shovelling the soil into a large bucket which was then hoisted up and tipped onto a lorry. This took a couple of days after which we set off empty up river, bound for the first National Rally of Boats at Market Harborough. Organised by the Inland Waterways Association, it was an unprecedented event which caused great excitement among the canal enthusiasts of the day and gained considerable publicity. Looking back, however, what should have been taken advantage of to interest merchants and manufacturers in the possibilities of canal transport turned out to be mainly dominated by the arty-crafty community. It certainly never resulted in any additional canal traffic.

Gerry Bird, of *Westminster* (the boat which had worked from Avonmouth to Newbury in 1947), assisted us from Oxford, a genial shipmate whose company I enjoyed. At Braunston I encountered for the first time the wide locks of the Grand Union Canal, and the tunnel there was the first long, wide tunnel I had been through. The short tunnels at Preston Brook, Barnton and Saltersford bore no comparison, and, while Harecastle was a long tunnel, you couldn't steer through it but had to let the boat go by itself.

To enter Braunston tunnel was to be confronted by an inpenetrable black wall, which the feeble rays of our headlamps did little to alleviate. John and Gerry, no doubt through lack of recent practice, found themselves unable to steer a straight course and our bows hit the wall on one side only to rebound onto the other. As soon as the steerer's eyes became accustomed to the darkness the throttles were opened, for it was possible to drive through these tunnels at full speed, slowing down only for oncoming boats. Before long a pin-point of light appeared ahead which grew steadily brighter. We eased down and hugged the wall as a pair of north-bound Grand Union's slid by, the combined noise of our exhausts reverberating in the dank cavern. Shadowy figures leaned on the tillers as we exchanged the time-honoured boatmen's greeting, "'Owd'yer do?"

Not far beyond the end of the tunnel we turned left onto the unfrequented Leicester Section of the Grand Union Canal. Ascending the flight of seven narrow locks at Watford, we entered the twenty mile pound, a lonely waterway along which we wound for hour after hour across an almost deserted rural landscape before arriving at the top of Foxton Locks, a flight with a fall so steep as to lay at our feet a wide view across the Midland Shires.

Foxton Locks were arranged in two staircases of five. Within each staircase the bottom gate of one lock formed the top gate of the one below. As boats could not pass in a staircase, the arrangement caused considerable delay in times of heavy traffic. My estimate of the capacity of these locks, based on three minutes operation time per lock and with boats going up and down alternately is only two boats per hour in each direction. The capacity of an ordinary flight of narrow locks is seven boats per hour in each direction.

Because of the staircase layout, the arrangement of paddles and side-ponds was not the same as we had been used to, but fortunately the lock-keeper appeared and showed us what to do.

The narrow locks at Foxton and Watford were the only obstacles to the operation of wide beam craft between the South Derbyshire coalfield, Nottingham and Leicester and the London area, the twenty mile summit having been built to wide boat dimensions. In theory the locks north of Foxton and south of Watford would accommodate barges of 14 ft beam but in practice such craft (which could carry 90 tons on a draught of five feet) appear not to have worked beyond Berkhamstead, although I was recently told by an old boatman that during the war they worked as far as the buffer depot at Cowroast.

Fellows, Morton & Clayton, who, in the 1890's were the principal carriers over this route, persuaded the Grand Junction Canal Company to purchase the Foxton to Watford section from its owners and to build an inclined plane at Foxton capable of taking 14 feet wide boats, the intention being to also widen Watford Locks. The plane was opened in 1900 and the boats were conveyed up and down in two tanks running on rails. The foundations proved to be inadequate and the low volume of traffic resulted in high operating costs. In anticipation of widening throughout, FMC had five new wide boats built at Leicester but sold them a few years later.

So ended an initiative which might have had far reaching results and it is interesting to speculate on the possible effect had a wide route been established between London and the Trent. By 1950 one would have expected it to be operated by motor wide boats, probably with mainly one man crews. These would have been about twice as economic as a narrow boat, even when the need to recognise the larger size of craft by paying higher wages is taken into account.

At the bottom of Foxton we turned right and followed the six miles of canal to Market Harborough where the basin was already full of boats. Among the many pleasure craft were a number of trading boats. There was Alf Best representing British Waterways South Eastern Division, Arthur Stokes with a resplendent pair of Ovaltine's, a pair of S. E. Barlow's and George and Sonia Smith with *Cairo* and *Warwick*.

There was a great deal of interest in the working boats but it was all concentrated on our traditional decoration and way of life. For instance, there was a prize for the cleanest boat, with the judges actually peering under the engine room floorboards. There was no organised attempt to sell canal transport at all, and, although I believe that the Rally coincided with the colliery holidays so that most of the boats would probably have been tied up anyway, their attendance at the Rally brought no benefit to their owners as transport is not sold by that type of publicity.

In its early years, the Inland Waterways Association was far more concerned with keeping open every last yard of the canal system than with the continuation of trade on those waterways which were still in use; to me its interest in working boats seemed to be overly concentrated on the traditional decorations and way of life of the narrow boatmen. Roses and Castles on the boats looked very nice, but I was reminded of the words of my next door neighbour when I was admiring the flowers in his garden. "They look well," he said, "but it takes a lot of them to make a boiling."

The IWA in fact, went so far as to actually oppose sensible cost cutting measures, such as the proposal in the last years of the nationalised fleets, to cut back the termini for some Birmingham goods (those that had to be delivered by road anyway) to Wolverhampton or Hawkesbury Junction.

The attempts that some carriers had made in the 1930's to improve productivity, sometimes met with little approval from enthusiasts. Even Tom Rolt, who, as an engineer, should have known better, described the innovative Tree Class motors of the Severn & Canal Carrying Company as being ugly and clumsy without mentioning that the design had achieved a 25% increase in carrying capacity over the more traditional type of boat. Of course they in no way resembled his ideal, which was a wooden, Oxford Canal horse-boat; and, within the fixed limits of length, beam and draught, any attempt to increase payload was bound to create a more clumsy craft, which would, when empty be more difficult to handle because of its reduced draught.

When Fellows, Morton & Clayton went into liquidation they were losing one shilling on every ton carried. Had they stopped building their heavy and old fashioned boats in the 1930's, when more modern designs became available, and gone over to vessels capable of carrying only three tons more per boat this loss would have been more than eliminated.

John was one of the judges in the Smartest Boat Competition, which prevented our boats from entering it, so I was spared the task of cleaning out under the engine-hole floors. As on most canal boats, the bilges were in a disgusting state, as well they might be because there was no drip tray under the engine and the oil could only be changed by letting the old oil run into the bilge. However, I kept our brasses, paintwork and scrubbed woodwork in pristine condition, spending much of the rest of the time helping George and Sonia who were operating passenger trips in their boats.

I had hoped that, when the Rally ended, we would go north via Leicester, the rivers Soar and Trent and the North Stafford. Instead we took the circuitous route via Braunston, where Bob rejoined us, Fradley, Haywood and Autherley. Not far above the top of Foxton we met a pair of loaded Joshers, a rare sight on the sparsely trafficked Leicester Section. The stern cloth of their butty was turned back for ventilation and the markings on their cargo of cases indicated that they were carrying tinned pilchards.

At Cut End we were joined by Ray White, who had bought an ex-Ovaltine motor which had so dismayed him by the way it leaked under its first load, (it had lain empty for a long time and the timbers needed to take up) that he had immediately sold it. Our first cargo was sugar, loaded at Anderton for Wolverhampton. On our way down after unloading we were going along in the dark with Ray at the helm, somewhere about Brewood, when there came a tremendous crash followed by an angry voice yelling "I'll put a shaft through that bloody light!" Apart from the occasional Cowpar, we were the only boats to be fitted with electric headlamps. All the others had oil lamps which were supposed to be lit after dark so that boats could be seen by oncoming craft. Boats with electric headlights, customarily switched them off when meeting other boats so as not to dazzle the steerers. The boat we had hit was the *Clee*, Captain J. Clowes, southbound from Knighton with a cargo of crumb. Fortunately we did not damage her as she was a nearly new wooden boat. The trouble was that, as her headlamp was not lit, we missed seeing her, the view ahead being obstructed by our high, empty fore-end; her Captain, in turn, was blinded by our light. After this, I got into the habit of using the headlight only when it was really necessary and leaving it switched off the rest of the time.

Ray, who had a propensity for creating catch-phrases, seized on Capt. Clowes' irate utterance with glee and the episode passed into the unwritten history of the John Knill Navy, to be lovingly recounted, again and again over the years to come.

On arrival at Weston Point our orders were changed to Ellesmere Port. Narrow boats, unless specially licensed, were not allowed to navigate the Manchester Ship Canal by themselves so one of the narrow beam Bridgewater Department tugs was ordered to tow us. Dwarfed by massive sea-going vessels, we found the journey, short as it was, very adventurous. Locking up into the basin at The Port we went alongside Frost's flour mill and started to load straight away, making Chester the same night.

At Chester we were joined by one of John's aquaintances, an old gentleman who had begged a trip with us. Feeling far from pleased, I had to give up my cabin and, together with Bob and Ray, had to pig it in the restricted space of *Kenelm's* accommodation.

Approaching Drayton Wharf, those of us on *Kenelm* were treated to an amazing sight. When a loaded boat met an empty one on the Shropshire Union it was necessary to ease right down and give her all the room you could, failing which the empty boat was likely to get stemmed up. John was doing something culinary in *Columba's* cabin and had left our passenger alone at the tiller. A group of empty boats – two single motors and a pair – were coming down the canal and we watched, open-mouthed, as *Columba*, ploughing along the middle of the cut at full speed, knocked them, one after the other, up the bank.

Columba heeled over as she struck the first boat, a saucepan of hot water sliding off the range and soaking John's trousers. The urgent need to remove them kept him out of the way below. Her headlong progress unchecked, she put the second motor up the bank, the old gentleman nodding benignly at the temporarily speechless boatmen, who were busy trying to rescue their far-flung mops, cans and cabin shafts. As the third motor took avoiding action and ended up with her fore-end in a field, an infuriated howl arose from its butty and a large formidable lady, flanked by two beefy daughters, appeared in the hatches. Sleeves rolled up to expose muscular arms, she seized her mop and brandished it in the direction of *Columba's* gallant crew.

We approached the disaster area with some trepidation. By now the boatmen, the first of whom was particularly large and of fearsome visage, had recovered sufficiently to start shaking their fists and promising all sort of interesting experiences to *Columba's* Captain and temporary crew who were now disappearing into the distance. Waving a placatory rope to indicate our intention of pulling them off the bottom we crept up cautiously, careful to dissociate ourselves in every way from "those learners up in front". Thankful to receive little more than glowering looks, we got them all afloat again and set off after our errant companion. John had fortunately suffered no physical damage but his temper was not improved by the incident.

Our passenger left us at Wolverhampton and I was able to move back into my cabin. While we were waiting to unload, Ray and I visited the offices of the LMR Boatage Department. The Stourlifters had just been withdrawn from service and we toyed with the idea of buying one. The office and dock was in Horseley Fields, an old-fashioned place where half models of various Shropshire Union boats adorned the walls. Although the name had disappeared in 1921, that part of the SU fleet engaged in collection and delivery work around the Black Country and Birmingham had survived, the boats then bearing the name of the LMS Railway. We had an interesting chat with the manager but didn't pursue the idea further. The thought of boating a horse-drawn SU boat up and down its home waterway was attractive but not very practicable. In any case the cheapest boat was for sale at £60 which we hadn't got.

After unloading at Broad Street and taking on oil and stores we set off once again 'down Shropshire'. For some reason that I cannot remember we stopped at Norbury Junction for several hours and Ray and I walked down the closed branch as far as Newport. The locks were still in quite good condition and we met a lengthman who told us that men still had to be employed to maintain the cut as a drainage channel and to trim the hedges. Our friend boasted a garden shed made out of the cabin of an old Shropshire Union horse-boat into which we were allowed to peep. At Newport Wharf, the warehouse still stood and it wasn't hard to picture the busy scene of bygone years. We were puzzled to be told that the last traffic had been "shit', until it dawned on us that this was the boatmen's straightforward term for the dried sewage sludge that used to be loaded at the Sewage Works Basin below Wolverhampton Locks and distributed as fertilizer.

While at Norbury, I must mention that there was another horse-boat at this time on the SUC. This was a family cabin boat which was used for transporting maintenance materials to places along the canal.

Once again we had orders to load salt but this time John had arranged to collect *Uranus* from her mooring at Middlewich, load her on behalf of Mersey, Weaver, and work her to the Potteries leaving her at their Burslem Dock. We had been debating what to do with her as, at that time, the salt cargoes seemed likely to continue and John preferred to operate them with two motors. John's newly purchased motor, renamed *Dunstan*, would soon be ready and could have made up a pair with *Uranus* subject to obtaining a crew.

The question of crews was difficult. To attract a reliable boat family from another firm was impossible unless you could offer them better boats or more attractive work. The sort of boatmen who changed jobs at frequent intervals, and there were not a few of these, were not a good bet for a small carrier who was likely to find an expensive pair of boats tied up without a crew at a trip's notice; and crews made up from unmarried boatmen were prone not to last long before splitting up. To crew single motors was very much easier; single boatmen were attracted to these because they would not be left in the lurch through being without a mate as was the case with a pair of boats. Another complication was the existence of various agreements between carriers not to poach each others' men. Even if a small firm did not subscribe to these it didn't pay to get on the wrong side of any of the large traders as they were a useful source of sub-contract work. Recruiting off the bank seemed the best plan. It didn't take long to train a boatman sufficiently well to get from one end of the canal to the other safely, if not with quite the speed and skill of the expert. There were, however, in that period of full employment, not many people looking for jobs on canal boats.

The four of us could have worked the four boats had John been prepared to work shorthanded, but, understandably, he liked his boats to have an adequate crew. For myself, I would have been glad to work a single handed boat having thoroughly enjoyed the brief experience of boating *Columba* by myself on the second salt trip. How things actually worked out you shall shortly see.

Just as poaching crews was frowned upon, so was there, in 1950, no competition for traffic between the canal carriers. In this respect, peace had descended upon the canal community after the cut throat days of the 1930s. It was a period when, for much of the time, there was ample traffic offering and sub-contractors were particularly sought after by British Waterways, North Western Division, whose management would have preferred to just take tolls and commission. BW tried hard to get the Potteries carriers to help out when they were busy, but without success. The only Potteries boat I ever saw with a BW cargo was John Walley's *Hawke* which made a trip to Sherborne Street.

Nor was there at that time, much competition with the Railways. The Rail/Road/Canal Conference provided machinery for fixing rates and the two forms of transport lived amicably side by side. The conference did not cover all road hauliers; there were many pirates. But, for what turned out to be an all too brief period, they posed little threat, being, at the time, quite uncompetitive on long distance, low value traffic and hindered from competing on many short runs by the sheer age of many factories, which had been laid out to receive raw materials by canal and to whose stokeholds and storage areas lorries were unable to gain access.

In obtaining the salt contract we had, ourselves, upset the status quo. Probably the railway didn't even realise, for a while, that we had abstracted this traffic which was small in relation to the total tonnage from Cerebos. When they did, they were to 'get at' the consignors to regain the work. The usual tactic was to quote a lower rate provided all the traffic went by rail. The rate could always be raised after the canal carrier had been put out of business. So stable was the traffic situation in 1950 that the only work that I recall being lost to the canal was the Worcester to Tipton and Ellesmere Port to Bloxwich flour jobs, lost in each case because of the destruction by fire of the consignees' premises, and the withdrawal of the LMR Stourlifters; BR having realised that goods could just as well be taken to the Western Region stations at Stourport and Kidderminster as to the London Midland Region Boatage Depots at those towns.

Leaving *Columba* at Anderton, we took *Kenelm* and *Uranus* to Weston Point and there received orders to load *Uranus* at Runcorn with felspar for Stoke. John went off somewhere leaving Bob in charge, assisted by Ray and myself. We reached Runcorn Docks by way of the Runcorn and Weston Canal, quickly loaded 20 tons and set off up Runcorn Locks, *Kenelm*, of course, remaining empty.

There was an unusual craft going up Runcorn in front of us, a British Waterways Wiganer, or Leeds & Liverpool Canal boat, piled high with crates of pottery ware. We had watched this being transhipped at Weston Point from some Knobsticks the previous day. The normal practice was to take this cargo over to ship's side at Liverpool on a Mersey flat, which would go down the Ship Canal to Eastham and then across the Mersey. Perhaps BW had found itgself short of work for its Wiganers and had organised this job for one of them; if they were indeed going to Liverpool the journey was not only circuitous but would have incurred Bridgewater Canal tolls between Runcorn and Leigh.

It is a matter of great regret that I didn't photograph this unusual movement. I had a cheap box camera but took very few canal photos, and those only of poor quality and little significance. Large scale interest in canal photography did not come until the last couple of years of the working boat era.

This was the first time we had been to Runcorn, a town which owes its existence entirely to the Bridgewater Canal and which was, in 1950, the home town of many boatmen and the headquarters of several carrying firms. Emerging from the top lock, we found the canal lined with boats, both those of the various potteries carriers and of the Runcorn coal traders. After boats had loaded or discharged, it was the usual custom to spend the rest of the day tied up here and to depart early in the morning. We, however, were going to press on to Anderton that night and, once clear of the aromatic delights of tanneries and gasworks were soon in the country and winding through the attractive surroundings of Norton Priory. It was nice to be back aboard *Uranus* and, with twelve lock-free miles to Anderton, we had a relaxed and easy day.

Next morning we proceeded to Middlewich, with *Uranus* towed by both *Columba* and *Kenelm*. It was on one of the sharp turns south of Lostock that, distracted by the sudden misbehaviour of *Kenelm's* engine, which had chosen that moment to run on only one cylinder, I got tangled up in some overhanging trees. No real damage was done as the chimney and cans were secured by safety chains but the incident provoked our Skipper to heights of fury.

It is an unfortunate, but nevertheless inescapable, fact of life that many an otherwise satisfying job is spoilt by poor personal relationships, a situation which arises more often when a small group of people live and work together at close quarters for long periods. The atmosphere aboard our boats had long been deteriorating and it was time for our ways to part. I arranged to leave the boats at Stoke-on-Trent, where there was a convenient railway station.

We loaded the two motors at Cerebos and had a trouble-free journey up Cheshire Locks and through the tunnel. It was the first time that we had worked a butty over this route and we were surprised to find that we went up very easily. Most of the locks are duplicated, that is there are two narrow locks side by side. *Uranus* was towed from her mast on the cotton line and, as the motor steerer went into one lock, he would take his end of the line ashore. After shutting the bottom gates and starting his lock filling, he assisted the butty into her lock by bowhauling. A loaded butty carries considerable way but the compression of the water in a narrow lock chamber prevents her from floating all the way in. The motor's lock would be full before the other one so that it was out of the lock and had the line at full stretch ready to start towing by the time the butty's lock was full.

After working up Cheshire Locks we understood why the local boatmen only put 20 tons on their butties and preferred the finely built local type of boat, which caused less resistance in the locks, to the bluffer designs favoured further south.

At Burslem we found some boatmen eager to earn the 'emptying money' for shovelling out *Uranus'* cargo so we left her with them.

Looking out of the windows of the train as it sped down the Trent Valley, I couldn't help feeling sad. Going boating had been the great adventure of my life and I had found it good. Now it was over for the time being, but I was determined to find some way of staying on the cut.

---------- CHAPTER SEVEN ----------

"DIRTY OLD COAL BOATS"

---------- • ----------

My arrival at home, jobless, was not exactly welcome to my family and I lost no time in trying to get back boating. Learning that George and Sonia Smith were on their way down the Grand Union Canal to Uxbridge, I went over there and found them unloading coal at the power station. They were working their pair two-handed and, when I explained my position, agreed to let me work with them for the time being. Full of excitement, I hastened back home, got my gear and was back aboard that evening.

Uxbridge Light was one of those small local power stations that were soon to disappear after the industry was nationalised. The coal was unloaded by means of shovel and wheelbarrow, most of the work being done on the night shift.

The next morning we awoke to find ourselves empty and so able to set off immediately. The boats were tied abreast and would remain so all the way to Cowroast, the summit of the long climb out of London and over the Chilterns. After having swept up the holds, rolled up the side cloths tightly and mopped off the coal dust, I got my bike ashore and started to lock-wheel. A bicycle was a useful thing to have on a boat so I had brought it along.

It was now September, a delightful time of the year for boating. A slight Autumn mist rose from the water as we set off, later to be dispersed as the sun rose. The temperature was pleasant without being too hot. The Grand Union Canal had a completely different atmosphere from the cuts I had so far been accustomed to. It was wide, deep and carried a heavy traffic, not only of narrow boats but also of barges which were to be met with as far up as Berkhamstead.

Passing Uxbridge Dock and numerous tied-up barges at the nearby wharves, we came to Uxbridge Lock which has only a shallow rise. The next lock, however, at Denham, is the deepest on the canal. Every time we met a pair of boats they would make some locks ready for us, the number depending on where they had met the last craft. When the locks were ready there was no need to lock-wheel, so this was important information to have. You therefore enquired, "Where d'yer meet the last?" or "How many've yer made ready?" and the steerer of the oncoming boat would either reply or hold up several fingers to indicate the number of locks made ready. It was vital to remember how many locks you had made ready yourself so as to be able to give this information to every boat you met. Every now and then we would meet a pair or a barge coming down which gave me a rest from lock-wheeling and a chance to have my breakfast.

When going ahead to the locks it was important not to get too far in front of your boats or a pair coming down might arrive at a lock you had drawn off before your own boats came in sight. Below and above each lock was a distance post, the first boat past one of these being able to claim the lock.

The whole tempo of working seemed to be much faster than that on the northern canals and I was to discover that this was not just an illusion caused by the boats being able to travel at higher speeds in the deeper water. Many of the boatmen were obsessed with 'Getting them ahead' and woe betide anyone who held them up. The offender was likely to be told 'get them out of the road or tie them up!' If he was being followed downhill when the locks were close together he might get 'drawn on', that is the following boats would empty their lock before starting to fill the one below. The lockful of water had nowhere to go except over the top gates of the lower lock where it would flood the cabins of the slowcoach occupying it.

Not everyone was a speed merchant of course. Many boatmen went about their work quietly, neither tearing along nor wasting unnecessary time. Instead of working on far into the night they would, when evening came, 'tie them to the side and put plenty of ropes out,' the last being a precaution against hard driving 'night-owlers'.

I had a lot to learn and could have had no better teacher than George who had been boating on the Grand Union all his life. We didn't call it the Grand Union incidentally. It was always The Junction after its original owners, the Grand Junction Canal Co.

Susan Woolfitt, in her book "Idle Women", gives a detailed description of the way boats are worked on the Junction. From her, I had understood that an empty pair was brought to a stand in an uphill lock by reversing the engine. George, however, used to get off with an uphill strap, a rope attached to the motor's anser pin (which is a shackle on the side of the boat at the rear end of the cabin) and stop the boats by taking a turn on a lockside bollard. He explained that this was quicker as, instead of having to jump up to the lockside off the cabin top, he was already up there ready to shut the bottom gate on his side. The position of the strapping post was such that the strap 'started' the gate a bit as it tightened. Sonia would get off, run up the steps on the opposite side and shut the other gate while I would draw, first the ground paddles and then the 'centres' or gate paddles. The result would be an impressive inrush of water as it boiled under our bows and we would be through the lock inside four minutes.

Our journey up the Colne Valley was through an attractive landscape, trees and fields being interrupted by the occasional industrial site which was old enough to be interesting rather than an eyesore. This part of the country had been a major source of raw materials for London's building industry. There were vast flooded gravel workings, one of which contained many sunken boats. Around Haresfield chalk and lime used to be loaded to boats, the flints which occurred in the chalk being sent to the Staffordshire Potteries.

At Rickmansworth, eight miles from Uxbridge, we passed Walker's Dock, birthplace of both *Cairo* and *Warwick*, and ascended the right hand of two locks, the other giving access to local wharves on the River Chess. Above the lock George pointed to some allotments and asked me if I knew that there used to be three locks at Rickmansworth. Sure enough the remains of a lock gate could be seen among the cabbages.

It should not be imagined that The Junction is an entirely artificial cut. Between Uxbridge and Berko much of it consists of the canalised waters of the Rivers Colne and Gade. I was told that there were places where, in time of flood, the current could flow so swiftly as to require two horses on an uphill boat.

A mile and a half above Ricky we came to the vast Croxley Paper Mill. A number of barges loaded with esparto grass and woodpulp were waiting to be discharged; among them some wooden craft of the type once used on the Upper Thames where they were known as West Country barges. A pair of BW boats was unloading coal while several more pairs waited their turn. Together with three others belonging to John Dickenson's, at Apsley, Nash and Home Park, this mill was the biggest single source of traffic on the Grand Union.

Not far above Croxley we entered the beautiful surroundings of

Casey (Cassiobury) Park, notable for the sharp bends in the cut, to emerge three miles further on at Hunton Bridge. Canalside industry now came thick and fast as, within three miles, we passed the Home Park, Nash, Apsley and Frogmore paper mills, the Ovaltine factory and Tooveys Flour Mill, all customers of the canal.

Around Winkwell the cut was lined with extensive watercress beds and here there was one of the few swing bridges on The Junction. Barge country was left behind at Berkhamsted, or in boatman's parlance Berko, and the towpath had been washed away above Dudswell causing lock-wheelers to take to the lanes to get Northchurch Lock ready. At last Cowroast Lock came into sight, the last of the uphill locks for the time being but offering only a three mile respite before we attacked the descent of the Chiltern scarp. Dropping down the seven locks at Marsworth, we tied up at 'the bottom of Maffas' outside a canalside pub and hard by the junction of the Aylesbury Arm. It had been an exhilarating day and, after a well-cooked meal, I retired to bed and slept soundly.

Locks came thick and fast in the early morning mist as we continued to drop down towards the valley of the Ouse. It always seems to me that this part of the country on the northern edge of the Chilterns has a special atmospheric quality. I like to think that Rupert Brooks walked here when he composed those evocative lines:

"White mist about the black hedgerows
The slumbering Midland plain."

The locks thinned out as we approached Leighton Buzzard where we passed the dockyard of L. B. Faulkner, one of the long-distance canal carriers. There are extensive sand beds at Leighton and we saw a pair of Harvey-Taylors loading that substance for Paddington.

Below Leighton is the infamous Jackdaw Pound abounding in sharp turns and lurking mud banks, followed by three locks close together at Stoke Hammond. Two more locks and another three miles brought us to Finney (Fenny Stratford) where a pair of Waterways boats were discharging grain at Valentin, Ord and Nagles while more boats unloaded coal at the gasworks.

At Finney I was given the motor's tiller for the eleven mile pound to Cosgrove. This can sometimes be a bleak, windswept part of the country, requiring one to be well muffled up in greatcoat and scarf, hunched down in the door-holes with a roaring fire in the range below you. But that day was pleasant enough and George got off at one point to pick mushrooms, rejoining us at the next bridge having taken a short cut across the field while we went the long way round.

These made a tasty addition to our breakfast next morning when we started from the top of Stoke Bruerne locks. Once out of the long Blisworth Tunnel I was again given the motor's tiller for the 16 mile pound to Long Buckby. A mile beyond Buckby Top Lock we came to Norton Junction where the Leicester cut went off to the right and from here I was again on familiar ground. We wasted little time oiling up at Braunston and were tied up at Sutton's in good time that evening.

There was the usual queue of boatmen waiting for orders when the Boat Control Office opened next morning. We were to load at Newdigate for Uxbridge and were fortunate, in those days of what were often lengthy delays in the coalfield, to be loading the same day.

Work was already well underway when we arrived at the Newdigate Arm and already the atmosphere was hazy with coal dust. The system of loading was the same as that I had previously encountered at Baddesley. While we were waiting our turn we rigged up our deck-boards and top planks so that when the coal had been loaded and trimmed all we needed to do was insert the 'uprights', (pieces of wood with V shaped notches in each end which support the middle of each plank) and pull up the side-cloths.

When *Columba* had loaded at Baddesley the amount of coal put on board had been limited by the shallow depth of the Birmingham & Fazeley Canal. Now *Cairo* and *Warwick's* loads were constrained by the cubic capacity of their holds and we had to pile the coal high in their 'back-ends' so as to get a good load on. When the coal had reached gunwhale height in *Warwick's* back-end, the slack boards, about ten feet long and high enough to bring the coal level with the cabin top, were inserted, their legs being pushed into the coal next to the gunwhales and the tops of the two boards tied together so that, when the intervening space had been filled up, they followed the tumble-home of the cabin side.

The hold of a narrow boat is divided into four 'rooms', known from the front as: the fore-end, back of the mast, stern middle, and back-end. Having piled the coal as high as possible in the back-end, it would still be above gunwhale level in the stern middle but, in a wooden boat, some boatmen would keep the back of the mast a little light, perhaps level with or below the gunwhales, going on to put a heap in the fore-end sufficient to bring the boat down level or just a shade by the head. Some grades of coal took up more room than others but all the coal boats southbound out of the Coventry Coalfield would be heaped up to a certain extent. This coal was all loaded in a dry state whereas, at most of the collieries around Cannock, the coal was washed before loading, making it much heavier.

British Waterways had a good many ex Grand Union boats with extra deep holds and on these the coal would be trimmed level with the gunwhales, their ample freeboard meaning that their side-cloths did not have to be used.

With the cargo trimmed to George's satisfaction we pulled out of the way of the dust and set to with mop and scrubbing brush to produce a smart and spotless pair of boats; after which we set off round to Sutton's where we topped up our provisions for the long trip south. I hunted out the nearest public baths, removed the last traces of coal dust and finished off the evening at the pictures.

The 23 mile stretch between Sutton's and Braunston is broken only by the three locks at Hillmorton and, once we had got clear of the first difficult turns, I spent most of the morning at *Cairo's* tiller. With a packet of cigarettes in the ticket drawer and the comforting warmth of the range at my feet I felt I could have stood on her footboard all day, the shining copper tiller in my hand and the length of the boat stretched out before me, obedient to every touch of helm and throttle.

A pair of Barlow's, just about to go into the dockyard arm, signalled to us that they had made the bottom of Braunston ready and in a few minutes the gates loomed ahead. I was about to be introduced to the method of working wide locks with a pair of loaded boats. The first thing to do was to get *Warwick's* 'uphill strap' out of the deck and attach the eye to her anser pin shackle, coiling the rest of the rope on the cabin top. We were towing on the 70 ft snubber and, approaching the lock, I went forward and, as George dropped the motor out of gear, coiled in the slack, making it fast when about twelve feet of rope separated the two boats. George accelerated towards the lock, aiming *Cairo's* fore-end at a slight angle towards the left hand wall about three-quarters of the way into the chamber. Just before it touched the brickwork he reversed smartly, the rotation of the propeller pulling her stern over so that she lay flush against the wall, coming to a well-judged halt with her bow fender (or bumper) just nuzzling the sill. *Warwick* slid into the lock beside her and, as her fore-end came abreast of *Cairo's* counter, George unhooked the tow-rope and threw the end of it over *Warwick's* mast plank. Letting *Cairo* tick over in forward gear he climbed onto the cabin top and hoisted himself up the lockside where he shut the bottom gate on his side of the lock.

Putting on *Warwick's* tiller strings to stop it swinging about and fouling the brickwork, Sonia seized the strap and stepped ashore, running up the steps to check the boat on the stump near the bottom gate. Having brought the boat to a stand she took a half hitch and a couple of turns round another stump situated further towards the top end of the lock. This was to prevent the butty from floating back and catching her helm on the gate, an accident which could, if unnoticed, sink a boat by holding her down as the water rose.

As George was now up by the paddles, I took up position to shut the bottom gate on the butty's side. As soon as it started to close George drew his ground paddle while I rushed up and drew the one on my side. We had to let the water rise in the lock a bit before we could draw the centres, which, as they admit water through apertures in the gates, would flood the boats if drawn too soon.

As the boats rose level with the lock-side the steerers stepped aboard, Sonia coiling the strap neatly on the cabin top and leaving the end ready to hand. A creak from the top gates as the weight of water in the pound above came off them signified that the lock had almost made its level. *Cairo's* engine was accelerated, pushing her gate open and, as her counter came abreast of *Warwick's* fore-end, George picked up the shortened tow-rope, took a half hitch on the motor's dolly to take up the strain on the rope as it started *Warwick* moving, then put the eye on the dolly and motored away up the pound.

This routine was repeated for each of the six locks at Braunston. We had a special short 'snatcher' for towing where the locks were close together, but, as a long pound followed the six locks, it was pointless putting the snubber away and getting it out again so we just shortened it up. At Finney it would be put away and the snatcher used from there to Uxbridge.

As with most operations on the cut, there are variations to this procedure. For instance, some boats were towed in the short pounds between locks by a rope going from the motor's counter, through a block on the butty's mast, then through two or three 'running blocks' which are D shaped pieces of wood fixed to the top planks, with a hole in them through which the tow-rope runs, back to a removable T-stud bolted through the cabin top immediately in front of the slide. The advantage of this method is that the butty steerer can take up the strain as the motor accelerates and pull the rope in when it is cast off. Against this is the nuisance of having coils of rope on the cabin floor, the possibility of getting your fingers caught, or jamming the rope and pulling out part of the cabin roof.

Old photographs seem to show that the overhead tow-rope was once the invariable method of working; but, by 1950, only a few boats used it. Was this perhaps a case of a new method of working being invented and almost superseding the old? Be that as it may, boats rigged up with all the paraphernalia of the overhead tow-rope were a fascinating sight; I longed to try my hand at this art but, regrettably, the occasion never arose.

Once out of Braunston Top Lock we let out the snubber to its full length and put away the uphill strap, getting out a more substantial rope known as the downhill runner. The black maw of Braunston tunnel loomed ahead and we plunged into its depths without slackening speed, George and Sonia steering a precise course down the middle. Considering that there is only 3'6" of water on each side of the boat when it is on the centre line of the tunnel, it takes quite a lot of skill to avoid bumping against the sides.

Buckby Top Lock came in sight and the downhill runner was attached to *Warwick's* anser pin shackle and left to trail in the water; as she swept into the lock alongside *Cairo*, moving at considerable speed because there is little resistance when entering a full lock, Sonia hauled up a bight of the soaking wet rope, leapt ashore, and quickly took three turns round the strapping post. Using the downhill runner required both speed and skill because the fast moving boat, with a gross weight of about forty tons had to be stopped in only about 15 feet.

George explained that the runner was dragged along in the water partly for convenience and partly because, being a long heavy rope, it would, if put on the cabin top, make a mess of the boat with the dirt it had picked up from the lockside. Dragging the downhill runner in the water had its disadvantages, however. When the cut was frozen it was painful to handle and, if for any reason it was necessary to breast up above a lock, in which situation the boats would be brought to a stand by putting the motor astern, it could, if you forgot to pull it in, get trapped in the closing top gates. This would often go unnoticed until the lock was empty with the result that it would have to be re-filled in order to extricate the wretched rope. It was embarrassing if any following boats caught you up while you were doing this.

Once the downhill strap had been used to check the butty it would be left lying on the lockside to be pulled into the water as the boat left the lock. The butty steerer, having closed the top gate, would take a length of light line attached to the stern stud, pass it round a handrail on the top gates and take it back to the hatches. He or she would then get back aboard. The flow of water through the bottom paddles would keep the boat forward in the lock until the levels were nearly equalised, then the boats would drift back to the sill. When this happened the string would be pulled in and made fast, thus preventing the suction caused by the motor moving out of the lock from dragging the butty out alongside it. The butty steerer would then step aboard the motor and, when the motor steerer had opened the bottom gate on the side, start it going out of the lock, immediately reboarding the butty. You had to watch what you were doing at this stage because the wash from the motor's propellor exerted a lot of pressure on the butty's 'elum in the confines of the empty lock chamber. If the tiller strings were to break, the great wooden tiller could swing across abruptly and knock you into the lock. More than one person has been drowned in this way. To obviate this possibility, many boatmen would remove their tillers when entering a lock, standing them up in the door-holes or laying them on the cabin top. George and Sonia didn't like their beautifully decorated 'elum to rub against the sill so we used tiller strings and had a neat little white fender attached to the rear of the 'elum to protect it.

As the motor left the lock, with the steerer dropping down onto the cabin top, the butty's fore-end would swing over into the motor's wake, and, with the motor steerer picking up the tow and his mate letting go the stern string at the right moment, follow the motor out through the one open gate.

The routine I have just described was the most commonly used way of checking the butty in a downhill lock. Another way of doing it was to put the strap on the butty's fore-end. The motor steerer would bring his boat to a stand, start his top gate shutting, step from the partly closed top gate onto the butty's deck as it went past, pick up the strap, get off at the middle stump (there were three stumps one each side of the lock) and strap the butty. He was then in a handy position to draw the paddles while his mate closed the other top gate. This was an excellent method and the one I adopted when, eventually, I captained a pair of boats down the Junction.

So far, I had managed this unfamiliar type of boating without making a fool of myself, but the next day, I was steering the motor round the Finney pound and was left to take *Cairo* into Finney Lock. We were, of course, towing on the snubber. I put *Cairo* into the lock in fine style, laying her flush against the wall in the approved manner; but by the time *Warwick* had drifted up to the lock, *Cairo* had swung across the chamber. I had not realised that I should have shortened up the snubber before entering the lock so that *Warwick* would be close behind me.

I had, in fact, a great deal to learn about boating. Working for John Knill, with our all male crew, we had had little contact with family boats and I knew little about the etiquette involved. If tied abreast of other boats you always walked across them in front of the cabin. You never went aboard the butty of your own pair without shouting, "Coming on!" and waiting for a reply. The mate was responsible for finding and chopping the firewood for both boats. If a swingbridge had been opened by a member of the crew of an oncoming pair, you didn't leave him to shut it but got ashore and did it yourself. I also picked up little tricks like kicking my boots against the side of the boat, so as to dislodge any loose dirt before stepping aboard, and 'starting' the gates with my back against the handrail at the mitre post end instead of pulling on the balance beam.

Beyond Finney we towed on the snatcher and, when there was no lock-wheeling to be done, I steered and strapped the butty. The technique of steering on such a short rope was to keep the butty to one side of the motor so as not to obstruct the flow of water from the propellor. To get round some of the sharp bends it was necessary to 'row the 'elum', that is, to push the tiller over as far as you could, letting go of it when it got to arm's reach, then, as the pressure of the water brought it back within your grasp, pulling it back towards you. This often had to be repeated until your arms ached. There was a good deal of sweating and struggling at *Warwick's* tiller for there were difficult turns in some places, particularly in the Parks. These usually had a concrete wall to prevent bank erosion, producing a nasty scraping sound if the unskilled steerer allowed his boat to drop down onto them. To allow a boat to scrape the side anywhere was considered to be very poor boatmanship.

On arrival at Uxbridge, the motor had to be winded in an arm just below the dockyard, about half a mile from our destination. The two fore-ends were then tied tightly together and we proceeded to the Light with *Cairo* going astern and *Warwick* steering both boats, a tricky task which Sonia made appear deceptively easy. George explained that the motor was then facing the right way to return to the coalfields when the boats were empty, the next winding hole being below Cowley Lock. While you were wasting time going below Cowley, you could be pipped by another pair of boats and lose a turn.

With an experienced Captain, who was tolerant of my ignorance, a good pair of boats, plenty of work and a well maintained route, boating with George and Sonia had a relaxed atmosphere and I was thoroughly enjoying it; but even better was in store.

When we got to Braunston, George was told that *Cairo* was due for her three yearly docking and we were to leave her there. Our change boat was to be the *Stirling*, a freshly painted Braunston built motor. To my great delight she had a Bolinder engine. I don't think George was quite so pleased. *Cairo* had a Ruston engine, a reliable machine with which he was quite happy. Its only fault was a propensity to excessive wear at the main bearings and, having put in two new crankshafts in about six years, Barlow's eventually sold it. I believe this problem arose because it was originally designed for use as a stationary engine. The Regent Oil Co used this identical engine as an auxiliary, driving a generator and air compressor, in their fleet of oil tank barges on the River Severn with complete satisfaction. Of course, the problem of crankshaft wear, expensive as it was to the owners did not affect the day to day running and its reliable starting and ease of handling was appreciated by the boatmen.

In my youthful enthusiasm I thought that having a Bolinder engined boat was marvellous and I longed to get my hands on the controls.

When we were ready to go George put the lamp on and started the engine and we crept cautiously out of the dockyard arm amid clouds of smoke and to the accompaniment of much banging and popping from the exhaust. I took up my position standing on the gunwhale that runs along the outside of every motor boat's cabin, expecting to be given the tiller after a while; but only half a mile beyond the junction the engine expired. George's brow grew black and he looked more annoyed than I had yet seen him. It occurred to me that even the most genial of men could be transformed by the perversity of inanimate objects. I don't remember exactly what the trouble was but it must have been quite serious as George decided we would have to return to the dock, which we did, bowhauling the boats stern first.

Our next attempt to leave for the coalfield was attended with more success and, with the boats well underway, George was once more his usual sunny self and explained the controls to me. Situated just inside the door-holes and under the cabin roof from left to right there were:

Manchester Docks

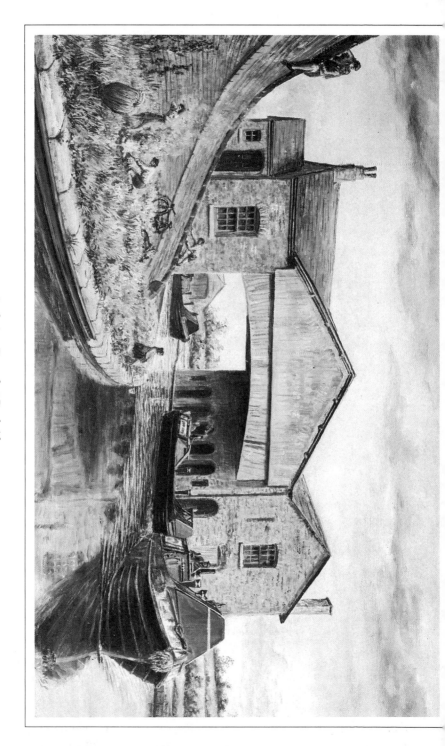

Anderton Bound at Barbridge

the reversing rod, speed-wheel, clutch rod and oil-rod. Having made sure that the engine was rotating in the right direction, to go ahead you pushed the clutch rod forward and turned the speed in a clockwise direction. The speed controlled a hit and miss governor. The engine ran steadily when it was full on, but turning back the speed produced that delightful rhythmic beat which is the distinctive hallmark of the Bolinder. The oil-rod opened the aperture of the injection apparatus which consisted of a brass spindle-case into which were screwed the jet and a moveable spindle. When the spindle was in the closed position fuel would emerge from the jet in a fine spray but, when open, it would come out in an unbroken stream.

You couldn't 'put the oil on' until the engine was well warmed up, otherwise it would cool the combustion chamber so much that the engine would 'go out'; and the oil had to be off before the engine could be slowed down on the speed-wheel. To reverse, the procedure was: oil off; speed off, clutch out; reverse rod back (at this point the engine revs would fall almost to the point of stopping before the direction of rotation changed); clutch in; speed on; oil on. The reader can imagine the amount of pulling, pushing and twisting necessary to execute any complicated manoeuvre, remembering that the steerer had his tiller and ropes to attend to at the same time.

The first and biggest impression made on me by *Stirling* was the tremendous vibration. Caused by the large single cylinder of an engine running at relatively slow revolutions (the maximum was 450 rpm), it seemed as though it was shaking the boat to pieces. It was impossible to stand a full cup of tea on the cabin top as it would slop all over the place.

While the engine had been running with the oil off, the exhaust had been smokey but as soon as the oil was put on the exhaust cleared as if by magic, the revs increased and the boat shot forward. A clear exhaust when opened out was one of the more pleasant characteristics of the Bolinder; Nationals were prone to smoke when driven hard, making conditions very unpleasant for the steerer.

Satisfied that the engine was now running properly, George gave me the tiller at Barby, but he took the precaution of remaining on the motor most of the way to Sutton's. This was wise because, had I met a pair of boats at a bridge-hole, I might not have succeeded in reversing the engine. I was enjoying myself and revelling in the satisfying rhythmic beat every time I eased off for a bridge. "Bomp bomp bomp bomp, bomp bo-bomp bomp" she would go, or sometimes "Bo-

bo-bomp bomp, bomp bomp, bomp bo-bomp bomp", until, with the speed wheel closed you got a slow, steady "Bomp......bomp......bomp ......bomp".

One of our companions that night at Sutton's was *Mabel*, which I had last seen at Banbury while we were doing the first salt run. She had been bought by a young couple, Mike and Polly Rogers who were using her to trade to Banbury and Oxford. It gave me great pleasure to think of this boat being brought back into trade rather than being used as a pleasure boat. Certainly she looked a picture, piled high with coal for Wolvercote, her paintwork unaltered except for the change of owner's name.

A feature of all Braunston built motor boats is a very long engine-hole, so spacious indeed that some families would put a bed in there or a cooking stove (to avoid messing up their highly polished cabin range). This was all very well, but the reduction in hold space meant that we couldn't get such a big load of coal on *Stirling* as we could put on *Cairo* when we went into Newdigate to load, once again, for Uxbridge. That night I resolved to get up first in the morning and show off by starting the engine.

As a youth I was always a reluctant early morning riser, but that morning I leapt out of bed with unaccustomed celerity. Stars shone from a chilly sky as I put my head outside but, once I had the blow-lamp going, I soon felt warm. When I thought that the hot-bulb had reached the right shade of cherry red I went through the routine of starting: oil on, three strokes of the fuel pump, oil off, another three strokes, pull out the spring loaded pin in the flywheel, foot on pin and kick. You had to remember to kick with the sole of your shoe and not with your instep so that the engine was less likely to hurt you if it kicked back. Your sole would slip off the pin more easily.

The first kick produced no result. I kicked again. Nothing happened. Another kick.......and another..... and another. The engine obstinately refused to come to life. After what seemed like an age a grinning face appeared in the engine-hole doors. "I didn't want to disturb you while you were enjoying yourself." said George. He cast an expert eye at the engine and explained that I had not had the lamp hot enough and had had it on for too long. While the firing pin in the hot-bulb had not got hot enough to ignite the fuel, the spindle casing had had time to heat up sufficiently to vaporise it before it was injected.

My embarrassment knew no bounds; but, eleven years later, the boot was to be on the other foot. I was then working on a barge on the Severn and was sent for to help two British Waterways fitters, no less, who were trying to start the ex FMC boat *Ling*, which had just been relegated to maintenance work and sent to Gloucester. Sure enough, I found that, just as on that morning at Sutton's, the blow-lamp hadn't been hot enough. As I kicked her nonchalantly into life, I felt that I had at last expunged my youthful disgrace.

The trouble with learning to boat was that, while the 'proper' boatmen were perfectly willing to teach you, they sometimes forgot that you weren't brought up on a boat and unconsciously assumed that you already knew things.

Later that morning, as we worked our way south through the damp green pastures of Warwickshire, my attention was caught by shouting and arm waving from the butty. I looked in the direction indicated and, there on the ridge above us, was a fox-hunt in all the glory of hunting pink, hounds giving tongue and the horses' breath condensing into clouds of steam in the cold air. In later life I came to disapprove of hunting but, in those days, it was not something to which I gave any thought except to enjoy the spectacle which, like the steam locomotives on the West Coast Main Line which paralleled much of our route, provided something different to look at, one field being much the same as the next.

As the day wore on I had my first experience of reversing a Bolinder, not, I hasten to add, that I was allowed to take *Stirling* into any locks. It was, however, necessary from time to time to 'chuck back' so as to clear the blades. Reversing a Bolinder is an art which requires both experience and confidence, both of which I lacked. If the engine is running in reverse there is a subtle change in its note. I couldn't detect this and left the door between cabin and engine-hole open so that I could see the flywheel. Lack of confidence means that, instead of waiting until the reverse action has actually taken place, you tend to restore the rod to its central position prematurely and the engine continues to run forward. It should be noted that the position of the reverse rod itself tells you nothing. Fortunately, for the purpose of chucking back it didn't matter if I made several attempts before getting into reverse.

There are other complications about the direct reversing Bolinder. If even slightly out of the correct adjustment the engine will 'go out' and it will do the same thing if it is allowed to get cold. For this reason the steerer must always have a strap ready when entering locks and be prepared to use it if necessary.

The problem of engines going cold could be dealt with in two ways. Normally a short external exhaust pipe would be used, but, in any situation where the engine would spend a prolonged time idling, this was removed and the "long pipe" substituted. There was also, on the engine, a handle known as the heater or damper which controls the intake of air for combustion purposes. It could be lowered to strengthen the mixture.

Whilst on the subject of additional controls I mustn't forget to mention the bracket, a handle on the engine which alters the stroke of the fuel pump. The bracket, and what the narrator did with it, features largely in all those stirring boating tales about overtaking or keeping ahead of other boats. In the last resort a desperate boatman would put some paraffin in a tin can and throw it in the buffer plates (the non return valve for the air intake) thus mixing paraffin with diesel oil and air.

We didn't need to resort to such heroic measures and *Stirling's* engine behaved beautifully all the way to Uxbridge, reversing perfectly at all the locks.

October was now upon us and, although George and Sonia didn't work very long days, we had it dark when starting, as was our wont, at six am. One morning, at the top of Stoke, I put my head out of the cabin to find *Stirling's* counter covered with the sparkling white rime of an early frost. The lock-keeper was already out, strewing ashes on the slippery gates and we trod with caution as we worked down the flight. Although there was no actual ice on the cut, my hands were soon blue from hauling the downhill runner up out of the water to strap *Warwick*. The smoke of our cabin fires rose high in the still air and the early morning countryside lay quiet around us.

Once out of the locks and into the Cosgrove pound, I coaxed *Stirling's* range until it was almost red hot, enjoying the grateful warmth at my feet and thawing out my hands on the chimney as I steered with my back against the tiller. The sparkling, frosty air seemed to invigorate us all. The engine took on a sharper note while the crew whipped up paddles and heaved on gates even more quickly than usual. Given a constant supply of cigarettes and cups of tea, and fed at regular intervals, I could happily steer and lock-wheel all through a long day without feeling the least bit tired; although, after we had tied up and sat down in the warmth I would quite often drop off to sleep, even doing so at the pictures. But then I was by no means the only boatman to do this.

On our third night out of the coalfield we had tied up below Ricky lock, waking to find our surroundings obscured by fog. "Thick as a bag!" grumbled George. Strangely enough this was the first fog I had encountered on the cut although winter fogs were far more prevalent in those days than they are now and quite thick fogs can occasionally occur on early summer mornings. The weather did not deter George, who lost no time in setting off, but we had to proceed with caution until it cleared. On this part of the Junction we were helped by the fact that most oncoming boats would be preceded by their lock-wheelers and we would see the barge horses well before we got close to their large and clumsy tows. In George's skilled hands a collision was unlikely and we arrived at the Light without incident.

We had already started our return journey and were in Uxbridge Lock when the lock-keeper came out with a message for us. We were to wind our boats and go to Brentford in order to load for Birmingham.

Before the formation of the Grand Union fleet in the early 1930s, the coal carriers had often worked back to the Midlands with cargoes supplied by Fellows, Morton & Clayton. This arrangement suited both parties as Fellows' had far more traffic offering from London than in the other direction and, by using sub-contractors, they could ensure that their own boats usually had a load each way. An amicable relationship existed as FMC were merchandise carriers and not really interested in the coal trade although their boats now and again carried a load of coal to a wharf at Uxbridge. Much of Josher's trade was in the carriage of foodstuffs and it is inconvenient to mix this with the movement of coal because of the difficulty of getting the holds clean and dry in wet weather.

The situation changed with the advent of the Grand Union Canal Carrying Company. The GU would offer back loading to the coal carriers and then deliberately delay their boats at Birmingham in the hope that the resulting shortage of coal boats might enable them to secure someone else's coal contract. As soon as Barlow's got wise to this tactic they simply refused all back loading until the coming of wartime controls brought them back into the north-bound trade. For a few years after nationalisation they relaxed a little and would take occasional back loads provided they had enough craft for their own traffic. Barlow's had survived the throat cutting of the Thirties but it proved to be the end of most of the Number Ones, who were forced to sell out to the large carriers, frequently having to dispose of their boats at knockdown prices.

This was the first time I had been to Brentford although I had cycled along the towpath from Uxbridge to Bull's Bridge in my early days as a canal enthusiast and I knew the towpath around Heston, North Hyde and parts of Hanwell Locks from my childhood. After passing Uxbridge Gas Works, where a wooden horse barge belonging to Thos. Clayton was loading tar, we locked down at Cowley, where the Slough Arm goes off on the right below the lock, and entered the long, lock-free stretch to Hanwell. This part of the canal was notable for its activity as waterside factories and wharves jostled for space on the canalside. The extensive timber wharves of West Drayton were followed by a roadstone depot. Tank barges lay at the Castrol Oil Works and coal boats were discharging at Nestles amid the delicious aroma of coffee. At Bull's Bridge there were more timber wharves, the junction with the Paddington Arm leading eventually to Limehouse, and the headquarters of the former GU fleet with its workshops, drydocks, slipways and an extensive lay-by where many boats were tied up awaiting orders.

Sailing straight past all this activity we came to Hanwell Top Lock. In this busy flight each lock had its own keeper who worked one side of the lock while the boatmen worked the other. The forbidding pile of Hanwell Lunatic Asylum, which had its own private basin, did not make Hanwell Locks the most cheerful place on the cut.

Emerging from the bottom lock we found ourselves at Brentford and were soon winding in a large basin amid a veritable armada of canal boats and barges. All round us were warehouses and the wharves were stacked with metal ingots and barrels. This was the busiest canal scene I had yet encountered. Apart from the through barge traffic which entered the canal here, Brentford was the depot for transhipment between barges from the Port of London Authority Docks and the narrow boats which traded to the Home Counties, Northampton, and the East and West Midlands.

Having tied up abreast of a pair of Grand Union boats, George went to the office and returned with our orders which were to load tomato puree for Birmingham on the following day. Having finished sweeping up *Stirling's* cabin and mopping off, I walked down to the Gauging Lock. It was tide time and a number of barges had arrived off the Thames and were waiting to enter the canal. As the first one nosed towards the lock gates, one of the lock-keepers threw the lighterman a rope which he dropped over one of his bollards. The other end was given a turn or two round a capstan and the cumbersome vessel was swiftly dragged into the chamber. When the lock was full the barge was given a good start out with the capstan, gaining sufficient way to float to its berth in the basin, or, if it was going up the canal, to carry it past the boats and barges, moored several abreast against the towpath, to where its horse waited to tow it onwards. The barge I was watching was loaded with wooden railway sleepers bound for the former Great Western Railway creosoting depot at Southall. This wasn't the only example of co-operation between rail and water transport at Brentford for a little way further down Brentford Creek was the Great Western Dock where lighters transhipped their loads from the docks into railway wagons. Walking the few yards from the lock to the bridge, I crossed the main road and looked downstream seeing yet more wharves, warehouses, boats and barges.

Returning to the lock I was surprised to see the familiar figure of Ray White standing on the towpath. Since I had last seen him at Stoke-on-Trent he had completed the third salt run, emptied at Reading, and loaded again with topsoil for Hampton Court, after which *Columba* and *Kenelm* had come down to Brentford and loaded for Birmingham. Apparently some difference of opinion with John Knill had resulted in an order to "get off at the next bridgehole" which he had promptly and literally obeyed, being not far from his parental home at Teddington.

Ray suggested that he and I should go to Bull's Bridge and ask for a pair of Waterways boats as we believed they had several tied up through lack of crews. This we did first thing the following morning. The fleet Superintendent at that time was a Mr. Wood who refused to employ us on the grounds of lack of experience. Ray pointed to our service with the John Knill Navy only to be countered with the mystifying remark "We don't work our boats like him." We never found out exactly what that was supposed to mean. As BW and its predecessor the GUCC Co. had employed trainees in the past after giving them a couple of trips with an experienced boatman, and we would be at least as well qualified as those so trained, neither of us, looking back on this episode thirty-five years later can account for our failure to obtain employment.

So it was back to Brentford where I found *Stirling* and *Warwick* just about to start loading out of a Thames Steam Tug and Lighterage Co barge. George and I were employed to stow the cases in our boats. The puree was in tins, packed in cases weighing about 56lbs each. A crane lifted a sling full of cases and deposited them on the floor of our hold where we placed them in position. Once the cargo had risen to gunwhale height each successive tier would be reduced in width. The object was to get as many cases on board as possible without making the boat top heavy. Tomato puree is relatively heavy as cased goods go but even so its bulk was such that there was no danger of loading the boats too deep in the water.

After we had put the planks and side-cloths up, Barlow's distinctive top-cloths were brought out. Unlike the shiny black tarpaulins of the GU or Josher's green canvas these were khaki coloured. With everything ready for our morning departure, I had a wash and set off to visit my maternal grandmother at Heston, eventually finding the 70 year old lady playing darts in the 'Master Robert", a pub on the Great West Road. Not having seen her for some years she didn't know that I had taken up boating and was quite intrigued.

The first couple of days of our journey northwards were accompanied by foul weather. It rained steadily up the long climb to Cowroast, and, as we were in a procession of Birmingham bound boats, we had only the occasional lock ready for us. Beyond Leighton the rain was accompanied by bitter winds, whipping unimpeded across the levels from the North Sea, and it was not until we were in the Northamptonshire Uplands beyond Blisworth that the weather broke. By the time we had passed Braunston it was dry and windless, with a hint of frost in the morning followed by wintry sunshine. In such perfect weather the entrance to the southern part of the Oxford Canal atNapton Junction looked so enticing that Sonia and myself, who were on the butty at the time, resolved to ask George if he would enquire for a load for Oxford when we got back to the coalfields.

The cut beyond Napton Junction was completely new to me. This was once the Warwick & Napton and Warwick & Birmingham Canals, which became part of the Grand Union system in 1929 and whose narrow locks were replaced by wide ones in the early 1930's. Experiments with the use of a motor wide boat, *Progress*, did not lead to the general adoption of these larger craft. Despite the wide locks much of the channel remained too narrow to permit wide boats to pass one another and they could not, in any case, reach the coalfields. Nearly all Grand Union boats arriving at Birmingham were required to return south with coal.

The lockage beyond Napton Junction was heavy, there being a long descent, through what was then sparsely populated countryside, to the valley of the Leam and an equally long climb up the other side. This included the impressive flight of 21 locks at Hatton where there was another Asylum wharf. I found the locks harder to work than those south of Braunston. There were no gate paddles, each lock having four massive ground paddles, totally enclosed and operated by a screw mechanism; the boatmen having to peer through a little window to see whether the paddle was up or down. The last five locks at Knowle were the heaviest of the lot and I was glad when we were out of them and in the ten mile pound to Birmingham.

There are three British Waterways wharves in Birmingham on the Grand Union and we paused at Tyseley, the outermost one, to find where we were to go. As we had expected the tomato puree was for Warwick Wharf, Digbeth, sometimes known as "New" Fazeley Street. To get there we had to pass the ex Grand Union depot at Sampson Road (they had bestowed upon it the imposing title of Birmingham Quay, but no-one ever called it that) and descend the six narrow locks at Camp Hill.

As our boats had been given a thorough clean up in the long pound above Knowle and George didn't want to get *Warwick* dirty going down Camp Hill, he told me to steer her with the shaft while he bowhauled and Sonia took the motor. As I had no idea what he meant, I got on and steered down in what, to me, was the usual way. I had never encountered the technique of shafting when working narrow locks and, in fact, didn't become acquainted with it for several years later. "I thought you knew all about working narrow locks," grumbled George without explaining what he wanted, not that there was time to do so as there was other traffic about. What I should have done was to draw a little paddle behind *Warwick* which would give her a start out of the locks, shut the bottom gates behind her and straighten her up for the next lock by pushing against bow or stern with the long shaft. This would have left the lock full for our motor which was following. We had never done anything like this when working for John Knill, nor had I yet observed anyone else using this method.

We had collected some mail at Tyseley amongst which was a letter from Ray. He had been offered a single motor on the Northern Road and wrote urging me to join him.

Camp Hill Locks are very dark and dirty, plunging beneath the Coventry Road and the main Paddington to Birmingham railway line to emerge at Bordesley Junction. To turn right here would bring you, via the filthiest cut in the Midlands, to the FMC dockyard at Saltley and to Salford Junction. This would be the route *Stirling* and *Warwick* would take to reach the coalfields when they were unloaded. We kept straight on, past the continuous line of wharves between Fazeley Street and the canal, until the tall and imposing new warehouse at Warwick Wharf heralded the end of our journey. Turning left into the basin we tied up amid a throng of other boats. It looked very much as though George and Sonia might have a few days enforced rest before getting unloaded.

After our mid-day meal I packed my things and said farewell to George and Sonia. They had been enjoyable company and I had learned a great deal on my few trips down the Junction; but I could feel the call of the Black Country and the Northern Road and it was with a feeling of anticipation that I walked out of the gates and headed for Sherborne Street.

CHAPTER EIGHT

NORTHERN JOSHER

·

When I had fallen in with Ray's plan to work a Northern boat between us, I had not really given the matter any serious thought. Although my·arrangement with George and Sonia was supposed to be temporary, we had all got on well together and they would, I think, have continued to find a mate useful for the remainder of the winter, although, as they pointed out, they didn't really work fast enough to afford one all the time. Low as a mate's wage was (£2 10s a trip on the Grand Union) it represented a considerable slice out of a boatman's earnings and the cost of food had to be added. The sort of people who really needed a third hand were those where the wife had young children aboard who required her attention.

When working for John Knill, as well as with George and Sonia, I had enjoyed the relatively luxurious conditions of good boats with electric light, plenty of food and regular wages. John Knill, who we had met somewhere along the Junction and to whom I had mentioned our plan, had warned me that to go Joshering was to endure the most primitive conditions and the possibility of considerable hardship.

The boat was to be a joint effort and we were to split the earnings 50/50. What should have concerned me ought to have been the possibility of future difficulties in our working relationship; Ray was to be Captain and, as the captain was responsible for employing the crew, I would not have the security of being on the British Waterways payroll. At the age of 17, I was still too young to have a single motor myself.

Such worries were far from troubling my head as I walked across the city centre towards Sherborne Street looking forward to the adventures Ray and I would have being able to paddle our own canoe away from the supervision of our elders.

It was about 4 pm when I arrived at the wharf and walked along the line of tied-up boats looking for *Eagle*. The afternoon was damp and rather chilly and I shall never forget stepping aboard and being welcomed into the warm cabin, cosy with firelight from the old-fashioned boat stove. Ray made a cup of tea and something to eat, while I put my things away and took stock of my surroundings.

All canal boat cabins have a similar layout but, instead of the 24 inch range I had been accustomed to, we had an "Eagle" boat stove, a bottle shaped contrivance on legs, with a hob, two draw-tins (one large, which covered the fire entirely, and one small) and a large ashpan. It will be remembered that FMC had only recently been nationalised and *Eagle* was as close to a pre-nationalisation Josher as you could get.

It had been a company which had kept a tight control over expenses. The Canal Boats Act forced them to provide a means of heating the cabin but, if the boatman wanted a range, he had to buy one himself. The only other thing the Act required a carrier to provide was a can for drinking water. Josher captains had to buy all their own ropes. Fuel oil and stores were strictly rationed and, if a boatman could not run his engine on the amount of lubricating oil issued, he would have been told to"take it to Saltley and tie it up." Until its last years a minimum number of crew on each boat had been prescribed, two on a single motor and four on a pair, and journey times were laid down.

All these restrictions had now gone by the board, but, so far, BW had been able to fit only a few boats with ranges, and electric light was completely unknown.

Eagle was an iron boat, built at Yarwoods in April 1926, and still bore her FMC livery, albeit the paintwork was a trifle faded. It is difficult to put into words, but the whole atmosphere of the boat was completely different from those I had previously worked on.

Looking round the boat I noticed that we lacked a long shaft. Ray wanted to set off without it but I knew this was impracticable. We could get stemmed up at any time and would be helpless without it. This meant a journey to Saltley dock in the morning. It was easy enough to get there on Birmingham's fastest trams, the "Washwood Heath Bogies", but to get the 18 foot long shaft back to the boat meant walking along the towpath, a lengthy and roundabout hike which took us first to Salford Junction before being able to point our steps in the right direction up the Eleven and the Thirteen.

Slinging the cumbersome object aboard with sighs of relief, we addressed ourselves to the engine which started easily enough. Bolinders do not have an oil sump, instead each bearing is fed from an individually adjustable pump located in a box of oil called the lubricator. For some reason *Eagle*, which was a Big Engine, sported a lubricator of the small size fitted to a Pup so we had to remember to lift the lid at fairly frequent intervals and top it up.

Ray took the tiller and I got down in the hold and started to splice on a dozen missing knee strings. Having rolled up the sidecloths to my satisfaction, I then put up the top planks, secured them with the girders and fitted the uprights, fiddling about until the top planks were exactly straight and level. We didn't have any brass chimney rings but had given the counter a good scouring and were rewarded, as we slid past the first tied up boats at 'Hampton, by a morale boosting compliment. "She looks better than when the last bloke had her," grunted a boatman, nodding approvingly. We went through the Broad Street bridge and tied up next to the *Trout*, a single motor worked by Ken and Vern Nixon, two of the fourteen offspring of 'Jumpabout Ernie', which was loaded with flour for Bloxwich.

During the time John Knill's boats had been working on the Northern Road none of us had got to know any of the boatmen at all well. Although they were always polite and helpful we were looked upon as outsiders and treated with considerable reserve. But now that Ray and I had the *Eagle* we were immediately accepted and made to feel part of the team. Other boatmen would often join us on board our boat for a yarn or a game of cards and, when tied up at Weston Point, we would be invited to take part in the evening games among the piles of material on the quayside.

Invited aboard the *Trout*, we were given a jam sandwich each and, as nobody had any money to go to the pub, we played cards for a while before turning in.

On *Eagle* we had only the barest minimum of cabin equipment. There was a Primus, a Tilley lamp and some basic cooking utensils. Ray had a sleeping bag on the cross-bed while I occupied the side bed, wrapped up in some old army blankets, the stove only a couple of feet from my head. I could usually look up and see the night sky above me because we left the slide open unless it was raining, in which case we would partially open one of the doors. I slept so soundly in those days that I never missed *Columba's* spring mattress which had been so admired by my friend Joe at Bodymoor Heath.

One memory that I have of boating was always waking up to a cold cabin. It was difficult to keep a range in all night unless you got up, raked and replenished it. A boat stove could be kept alight by placing a 'banker' on it, a piece of large coal with the grain running horizontally, but such coal was difficult for us to obtain.

Next morning we went round to Albion Wharf for our 'starting money' and stores. The starting money was £1 and was deducted when you 'settled' at the end of a trip. Stores consisted of lubricating oil, lamp oil, meths, a handful of grease and another of soft soap each wrapped up in a sheet of newspaper, asbestos string and two wipers. If you had used your spare cylinder head joint, or gasket, you could draw another one. The asbestos string was for making joints (where it was smeared with blacklead) and for packing the spindle. Water pump and stern gland packing was issued as required. You were expected to do most of the engine maintenance yourself including the replacement of blown joints. Rope was also issued. We needed a strap but, in this period of post-war shortages, the depot hadn't got any of the right size of rope. I had already noticed that some boats were having to strap with a length of doubled up line. Another thing that was unobtainable was a proper water can. Instead we were given a thing resembling a small milk churn.

By the time we had got ourselves organised, it was afternoon when we started to go down 'Hampton Locks, with me steering and strapping as it had been arranged that I should steer in the downhill locks and Ray in the uphill locks. Neither of us had ever used a gate strap before but I quickly became accustomed to it and soon we were going down the locks hell for leather.

As we went in each lock I dropped the boat out of gear, stepped off the counter with the end of the strap in my hand and took a couple of turns round the strapping post which projected from the breast of the gate, calling out "Draw!" at the same time. Holding on to the strap I stepped onto the footboard of the gate which was rapidly closing under the combined action of strap and paddle, and rode the gate across to the other side where I dropped the outside paddle and draped the strap over the tiller ready for the next lock. Ray tied the boat down using the tack string attached to the mast. If he had to go down to get the next lock ready I would draw the other bottom paddle and open the gates, kicking the outside one open first, before jumping down onto the cabin top and driving out. Lock after brick-dripping lock was left behind us as Wulfruna's smoky chimneys gave place to open countryside. Dusk was falling at Cut End, enhancing that remote, mysterious atmosphere that was so characteristic of the Shroppie.

As we plunged into the darkness of Chillington Woods a tiny spark in the distance heralded the approach of an oncoming boat and soon we were abreast of its horse, plodding stolidly through the gathering gloom towards its night's rest at Autherley. A dog barked briefly from the deck of the loaded Thos. Clayton and, as the almost barbaric paintwork of the cabin slid by, we could see the array of brasswork and hanging-up plates through the open cabin doors and smell supper cooking on the gleaming black range. A stout, middle-aged lady gave us a grave "How d'ye do?".

That night, after we had tied up at Wheaton Aston, we were joined by Freddie Morton with the *Mendip*. Charlie Atkins, with whom this boat is always associated, had the *Clent* at that time. Fred had come, singlehanded, from Audlem Town Lock that day, putting our day's journey to shame.

It was hardly to be supposed that we should get 'down Shropshire' without getting stemmed up, nor did we. Fortunately we had hardly been struggling with our long shaft for five minutes when along came the *Chiltern*. Her steerer, a taciturn little man who we knew as 'Bandy', took a large black pipe out of his mouth only long enough to grumble "I'm boating this boat, not yours!," in reply to our request for a snatch, but he delved inside his cabin, producing a strap which was obviously too precious to be kept anywhere else and pulled us off the bottom before turning his back firmly on us and shoving in his oil-rod. Not always the most sociable of characters, he was, however, known to unbend occasionally, and was both a fine boatman and, I later discovered, a wizard with a shovel.

We lay at Barbridge that night and, on reaching Middlewich the next day we paused to buy a stick for making a mop. For this purpose, a six foot long ash stale, or handle, was necessary, the end of which was bound with an iron ferrule. A hole was bored in it with a red hot poker to take the six inch long, square sectioned mop nail, on which strips of cloth cut from an old overcoat were threaded between two small squares of leather. Having mopped off you could get the water out of the mop by rolling it down your arm to make it spin rapidly, an art which took some practice. It was known as 'trindling' or 'strangling'. With the dry mop you could remove the excess moisture from your woodwork.

The cratch had to come down when we got below Middlewich because of the low bridge in the Big Lock Pound. At the Lift we had orders for Weston where we arrived after an uneventful day. There were a number of boats already there, including the Shaws with *Cypress*, *Madeley* and *Shad* Arthur Harris with *Perch* and Harry Barry with *Otter*, and we were joined, the following day, by Bill Wain who now had *Arabia*, Ike Wilson having given her up to take on a pair.

We re-erected the cratch taking great pains to get all the wrinkles out of the deck-cloth which, as it was already faded, we scoured with a solution of alum to make it snowy white. Then we settled down to wait for a cargo.

Trade was temporarily very slack and it was several days before we got any orders. During the daytime we would chat with the other boatmen, do little jobs around the boat and stroll round the dock or go to the chip shop. *Madeley's* fore-cabin was abreast of our stern and Mrs. Shaw's two daughters, Evelyn and Emma spent much of their time in it reading comics. Ray also bought a comic, the first issue of the EAGLE, which contained an illustrated article about the aircraft carrier of that name.

When dusk fell there was more serious business afoot as shadowy figures could be observed slinking round to the other side of the dock where a steam dredger was tied up, returning later with a bag slung over their shoulders. Coal, and how to get it, was one of the main pre-occupations of Shropshire Union boatmen. On the London Road, coal was the principal cargo. There, most motor boats had a bunker in the back-end kept full of coal which also served as ballast to keep the stern down when running light. Even if the coal you were carrying was unsuitable, you could pick up coal that had been spilled at the loading places or get some off another boat.

The only coal carried on the Shropshire Union was to Cadbury's at Knighton and this didn't move in our long distance boats but in Joey boats belonging to Ernie Thomas. Coal was brought down the Trent & Mersey to Seddon's at Middlewich but, as it was nutty slack, you needed time to pick the nuts out. The coal carried on the Duke's Cut was nearly all too small to be useful but, if you knew one of the boatmen, he might give you a bag of nuts scrounged from the colliery. The coal supplied for steam dredgers and for the steam cranes that unloaded the spoil was regularly raided.

On the BCN, the crews of Joey boats might sometimes have time to throw you a lump or two or scoop a shovelfull of nuts into your hold when you met them. Stewarts & Lloyds boats, which carried DS nuts, regularly tied up at the top of Tipton Factory Locks and if you could arrange your journey to stop there overnight this was a good, quiet place for topping up supplies. A favourite ploy on *Eagle* was to go round the 'Hampton Pound in the dark, there being a coal wharf at Bilston at which a Joey boat full of house coal was nearly always moored. It was a dark place but you had to be careful as there was a nearby bridge and a copper might be peeping over. At Winson Green, a stack of railway coal spilled through the railings and could easily be picked up, but it was of poor quality. Northern boats didn't have a back-end bunker, having instead a shelf under the back-end beam, so even when you could get some coal the amount you could store was limited to a few sacks full. A range could burn a bucketful of coal a day and a boat stove somewhat more. Somehow we managed to keep ourselves supplied on *Eagle* and we always had a fire; but it was not unknown for boatmen to break up the cabin drawers in order to have something to burn.

Had we been working for Fellows, Morton & Clayton we would have received no wages while we were tied up; but BW paid laying money of 10 shillings per boat per day after three days' waiting time had elapsed, and there was a fallback of £2 10s per boat per week, If you ran out of money you subbed, or drew an advance, which would be deducted when you settled at the end of a trip. I don't have the exact figures but we earned about £5 10s between us for a trip from Birmingham to Weston Point and return, to which stacking and hanging-on money would be added. We put £1 2s 6d each into the kitty for food and lived comfortably on it; there were, of course, no rent, rates, lighting or heating bills to pay. Both of us drank only on rare occasions and I smoked perhaps five or six cigarettes a day.

In theory, a round trip a week was not difficult to do. However, delays waiting for orders and for unloading, and those caused by the canal freezing in winter, reduced the performance substantially.

After spending several days at Weston, orders came out for Harry Barry, Arthur Harris, Billy Wain and ourselves to go empty to the Potteries, there being two loads of gravel for Manchester and two loads of coal for Middlewich. Hastily getting aboard a supply of food and fags, lamps were put on and engines kicked into life. Up the Weaver we went abreast of *Perch*, Arthur complaining that our Big Engine wasn't pulling as well as his Pup. This was partly because someone had told Ray that if he had the bracket up more than half way he would run the big ends out, and partly, so Arthur assured us, because our clutch was slipping. All four of us tied up above the Lift where Arthur offered to fix the clutch for us, after which we all went up to the pub.

It was assumed that the first boats to arrive at the Potteries would get the choicest orders, that is, the Manchester loads. Accordingly, Bill Wain and Arthur crept off very early in the morning without calling us. *Otter* and *Eagle*, both of us having Big Engines as against the Pups of the other two, followed in haste in the hope of overtaking our rivals in the deep water of the Big Lock Pound; but our clutch was now slipping very badly and we had to tie up at Broken Cross and adjust it. Obviously Arthur had perpetrated a typical boating trick to make sure of being first. This delay meant we had it dark going up Cheshire Locks, and as most of them are duplicated, two locks side by side, the lock-wheeler had to take a torch and exhibit a light to indicate which of the two locks he had made ready. We had no headlight, not even an oil one.

Our companions had already gone through the tunnel but we had to wait for the first tug of the following day. There were several boats waiting and some of the other boatmen showed us how to rig up a plank in such a manner as to protect the right hand corner of our engine-hole. This was essential on an empty boat as it was impossible to steer and, in one place, there was an abrupt 'step' in the tunnel roof which would otherwise catch the engine-hole and do enormous damage. John Knill wouldn't take his boats through Harecastle when they were empty but Joshers had to do it regularly.

Reporting at Mersey, Weaver's office next morning, we were surprised to find that Arthur and Billy had already gone to Sideway to load coal and we were to have the gravel. Our rivals had forgotten that, in the Potteries trade, the otherwise universal practice of first come, first served did not apply, boats being loaded or unloaded in the same turn as when they were given orders. Presumably *Otter* and *Eagle* had been specifically ordered for gravel.

The gravel loading wharf was right next to Mersey, Weaver's office at Longport. We followed *Otter* into the length but had to wait until afternoon for our load which was brought in three lorries each carrying six to seven tons. At one time boats had gone down to Trentham to load, but it had been found more convenient, since the gravel had to be put into lorries anyway, to bring it to Longport.

One after another the lorries backed up against the baulk of timber at the edge of the wharf and tipped their loads into our hold. Having no idea how to distribute the load we ended well down by the head. By the time we were loaded it was dark and having, quite unnecessarily, pulled up the side-cloths as far back as the mast, we started to trim the chippings back by the light of the Tilley lamp which we stood on the mast-beam. Before long, an angry shout reached our ears which turned out to have emanated from Mersey, Weaver's owner and manager, Mr. Shirley. Purple faced, he materialised on the wharf and accused us of throwing our cargo into the cut. It was a common enough practice to make his suspicions reasonable and we had some difficulty in persuading him that we were merely trimming. Picking up the Tilley lamp to show him our fore-end which was "in the paint" as the saying goes, we discovered that it had burnt a small hole in our sidecloths just above where it had been standing.

This incident prompted us to make up another verse for the poetic saga of boating life we had been composing.

"I remember, I remember, how Shirley did his nut
Because he thought he'd caught us throwing chippings in the cut.
The Tilley Lamp upon the beam revealed us to his gaze;
When we turned round, guess what we found, the side-cloths all ablaze."

For once on the cut sweet reasonableness prevailed and the gaffer went home happy to his tea while we started up and went to the tunnel, passing Billy Wain who had decided to spend the night at his home port of Tunstall. *Perch* and *Otter* had gone through the tunnel and were, no doubt, well on their way down Cheshire Locks, but, once again, we had to wait for the first morning tug.

At Rode Heath next morning we lost our cooling water and had to stop. All canal boat engines of the period were cooled by pumping raw canal water through the engine, debris being excluded by a grid over the intake and most of the sediment trapped in a mud-box. Unscrewing the cover of this and removing handfuls of slimy mud was a regular chore. Cooling systems were a frequent source of trouble and a steerer would keep a constant eye on the outlet, fearing to see the tell-tale cloud of steam. The first thing to do was to take the 'boat's bottom brush', used for sweeping up the hold, and rub it up and down over the inlet grid to clear it of any obstruction. This had no effect so we opened up the mud-box. It had very little sediment in it but, on re-opening the sea-cock, no water flowed through. The blockage was therefore between grid and sea-cock. We were afraid to take the sea-cock valve out of its seating in our loaded condition so we had to send to Northwich for a fitter. He made short work of the trouble but we were now well behind the other boats.

So far behind were we that we met *Arabia* at Middlewich on her way back to Sideway, Billy having arranged another load of coal. After we had got to Manchester and unloaded at Trafford Park we went round to the top of Hulme Locks where BW had an office and settled down to wait for another cargo.

Ray and I took the opportunity to explore the Rochdale Canal as far up as Piccadilly, a waterway that is even more secret and enclosed than the BCN at Farmers Bridge. A daily Wiganer still went up a few locks to a small power station in the city and, very occasionally, narrow boats took salt up to a depot at Piccadilly Basin. Most regrettably, Manchester had made the foolish decision to do away with its trams and the last one had recently ceased to run; but there were still some in Stockport, to which town we repaired for an orgy of tram riding. Later we found a particularly palatial public baths and were persuaded to visit a pub in Hulme much used by boatmen and flat men, where we were introduced to the Manchester dart board which has doubles and trebles much narrower than the size to which we were accustomed.

There were rumours among the assembled boats of a consignment of imported cheese for the Midlands, by which Northern boatmen meant Nottingham or Leicester, but whether it ever materialised I don't know. *Otter* finally had orders for Ellesmere Port and, not long afterwards, we were sent empty to Weston. Dusk was falling as we approached Runcorn, and, although we weren't very familiar with Runcorn Locks, we pressed on down them in the dark.

At the place where you turn off into the docks I was horrified to find that I was heading straight for Mersey, Weaver's *Dee*, with her piled-up load of acid-filled glass carboys, which was tied up broadside to us. Turning off the speed and pulling the clutch rod out, I hauled back on the reverse rod and was rewarded by an instant reverse. Banging the clutch in, I turned every thing on and, water boiling under the counter, brought up with only a few inches to spare. Breathing a sigh of relief, I spotted *Otter* tied up some way ahead and we laid *Eagle* alongside her.

No sooner had the last notes of our exhaust died away and we were engaged in setting up our fore-end and stern strings, when Mrs. Barry appeared in *Otter's* door-holes. She was in tears. "They've taken my Harry away" she told us. We did our best to comfort the distraught woman and, finally a coherent story emerged. While *Otter* had been waiting at Runcorn for the tug to take her to Ellesmere Port, she had had a visit from the police who had arrested Harry and taken him to Nantwich jail. More we didn't know for the time being. Mrs. Barry was very upset. They were a devoted couple and, with typical insensitivity, she had been left alone with the boat, with no-one she knew to hand, for the Barry's did not come of old boating stock.

Obviously *Otter* could not now go to the Port so we took her into Weston where there would at least be other Joshers. The Runcorn and Weston Canal being closed for repairs, we once again locked out onto the Manchester Ship Canal where a tug took us, together with a pair of Mersey, Weaver's, to Weston Point.

Here it was decided that we should load *Otter* and help Mrs. Barry work her to Barbridge, by which time it was hoped that the police would have completed·their enquiries and have released Harry. Having loaded 20 tons of spelter apiece, we went up the river abreast and tied up below the Lift. When we emerged from the Lift in the morning we encountered two more women whose husbands had been arrested. They, however, took it all very lightly and joked that, while their men were away, they would take the opportunity to go on the game. One of them, who we knew as Black Aggie, eyed Ray and me speculatively, while her teenage daughter, who was standing behind her, rolled her eyes and made a gesture of derision in the direction of the adventurous pair.

At this point, a young lad who had been standing on the towpath, intervened. " 'Ow much am yo' gooing ter charge, Missus?" he ventured. "I orter get half price 'cos I'm only thirteen."

The mood of the ladies swiftly changed from light-hearted badinage to anger. As one seized her mop, her crony hurled vituperations at the intemperate youth. "I'll shove two fingers down yer throat an' pull yer liver out!" she promised. The boy retreated to a safe distance and broke into the opening verse of the curent popular ballad. "They've locked up my lover in Allantown Gaol." he wailed, "oo, oo, oo-oo."

The brows of the women darkened and brawny biceps rippled menacingly as they delved yet deeper into their repertoire of abuse. "You'll be gooing Oo! when I tell yer Mam, yer snotty-nosed little bleeder." yelled Aggie. We could still hear the lugubrious wail, "They said at the Courthouse he'd never go free, ne-ver go free," as we shoved in our oil-rods and disappeared round the bend.

Off we went round the Big Lock Pound with myself in charge of *Otter* while Mrs Barry made our breakfast porridge. We met Harry walking along the towpath near Chumston and promptly tied up for the night above the lock.

Over cups of strong tea, sweetened with condensed milk, Harry told us his story. Certain boatmen (we were later to discover that nearly all the boatmen in the Northern Fleet were involved) had been selling copper to a lock-keeper on the Middlewich Branch who acted as a middleman for professional crooks in Manchester. The boatmen had been paid a mere 10 shillings per half hundredweight ingot. The crime had come to light and the police had arrested everyone concerned and held them while they made enquiries.

From Chumston we made our way steadily southwards, pausing at Audlem where there was a shop that sold clogs. They were in common use on the North-Western canals and I was determined to have a pair. Clogs are excellent for working in but you have to become accustomed to walking with your foot held a little stiff.

The Shropshire Union was, in those days, noted for its large population of herons and, as the long, straight levels could be a little tedious, watching them helped to pass the time. The birds would stand still until the boat was nearly up to them and then take off and fly a little way up the cut in front of us, stopping again to let us catch up. You could never overtake them, they would always take off as the boat drew near. I think that the movement of water in front of the boat caused the fish to rise. The herons had discovered this and knew where to look for their meal.

The towpath was lined with telephone poles and another diversion was to bet on how long it would take the boat to reach the next pole.

As far as domestic matters went, we had a comfortable routine. Ray cooked the breakfast porridge; rationing was still in force and this was one of the few plentiful foods. I cooked dinner, which was usually luncheon meat, mashed potatoes and tinned peas. We had no culinary skills nor ambitions and, in any case, had only the open fire of the stove to cook on. Sometimes we would have a tin of steak and kidney pudding which was a favourite treat. Our cheese ration was made into cheese-dip by slicing it up and melting it with water to which pieces of bread were added. I didn't know it at the time but this is, in fact, a traditional Shropshire Union dish. Eggs and bacon were welcome but the ration was tiny. The fish and chip shop was a godsend to boatmen and we found them to be much cheaper in the North than they were south of Birmingham, a large portion of chips at Middlewich costing just tuppence.

There was little chance of increasing our food supply by pilfering from the cargo. The only foodstuffs regularly carried by our fleet were sugar, flour and chocolate crumb. We never encountered any of the occasional cargoes of canned foods or imported cheese and had we done so we would have let them alone. Two boatmen had recently been successfully prosecuted for selling cheese at Leicester, and notices to this effect were displayed at various canal offices.

From Chumston we made Knighton and were tied up at 'Hampton by 4pm the next day. "Come on, you can't stop here, you're supposed to be going to Birnigum," joked a boatman, but we had our own plans. We were going to visit the laundry, get some shopping and then set off round the 'Hampton Pound later in the evening. About seven o'clock we started and, as we approached the coal wharf at Bilston we were glad to see a loaded boat tied up there. We drifted slowly alongside it and stopped, Ray holding the boats together while I transferred a useful quantity of large house coal to our boat. A couple of minutes later we pushed ourselves quietly under the bridge before opening up the engine. With a roaring fire under our feet we had an enjoyable journey in the dark to Sherborne Street.

Both of us agreed that the night time passage of the Wolverhampton Pound was one of the most enjoyable parts of boating; and I knew one or two other young boatmen who felt the same way. The deep water twisted this way and that in its dark canyon of buildings, emerging, beyond the steelworks at Spring Vale, to give views of the Dudley ridge, upon which the street lamps (which were white in those days) sparkled like stars.

For both of us, products as we were of the Home Counties, the Black Country had the same fascination. If it was no longer the Gehenna of Victorian times, it had yet to become the Golgotha of the 1980s. Although the continuous smoke and flame of primitive industry which once covered the area had disappeared, much of the flavour of an older age remained. By day, a thousand fuming chimneys flaunted their sable banners, while the night sky was still riven by sheets of flame. The great steelworks of Bilston, Wednesbury and Round Oak still stood, surrounded by their acolytes of forge, rolling mill and machine shop.

Through this jumble of towns, villages, factories, brickworks, wasteland, cinder tips and marl-holes ran the Birmingham Canal, its murky waters still bearing upwards of 200 loaded boats each day. A network of railways contributed the exhausts of many steam engines to the smoke laden air as the wagons pursued their intricate path, wheels grinding and squealing on the sharp curves, through a maze of iron byways to reach sidings remote from any main line.

Now the piles of smoke blackened brick where men toiled before the furnaces are almost gone as are the canal wharves and the sidings. Instead there have grown up characterless acres of industrial estates of a tedium unrelieved by any features of interest. The services of innumerable lorries are needed to service these soul-less places, resulting in the construction of vast carpets of concrete and asphalt to carry them, to build which demanded the dispersal of whole communities. The tower blocks which replaced the 19th century slums have themselves, in a few short years, become slums.

Truly, the planner of today could say, with Ozymandias, "Look on my works ... and despair."

There was a whole crowd of boats at Sherborne Street and no chance of unloading the next day. After a leisurely breakfast we stacked our spelter and visited the public baths and the barbers, returning spruce and shining for our first date with a couple of boat girls.

These were none other than the two hefty wenches who we had encountered at Market Drayton when we had been working for John Knill. While we waited in eager anticipation, they took their time preparing themselves for the evening, finally emerging from their cabin with their hair sculptured into improbable shapes, achieved, they assured us, solely with the aid of water. Off we went to the local fleapit. My date was the youngest of the two sisters, a girl of rosy features and pillowlike bosom, which, being very inexperienced, I was quite content to be allowed to explore, in the darkness, only outside her dress, further intimacies being firmly repulsed. As was customary, we walked home eating vinegar-fragrant chips out of sheets of newspaper.

A move to persuade the young ladies to come aboard our boat "for a cup of tea" was still-born. The grim features of their mother appeared above her door-holes as we walked along the wharf and the girls scuttled aboard their own boat like startled rabbits. I thought I detected the faint ghost of a knowing grin on the old lady's face as we bade her goodnight.

As soon as we were empty we had immediate orders for Knighton. Calling first at Albion Wharf for fuel, stores and to settle, we laid in some rations and, picking Jim Beady up at the Top Lock, went down and tied up at the Cut End.

Putting our heads outside next morning we found our surroundings

Land of the Knobsticks

THE NORTHERN ROAD

MANCHESTER

LIVERPOOL

Manchester Ship Canal

Bridgewater Canal

Runcorn
Weston Point
Preston Brook
Ellesmere Port
Anderton
Weaver Navigation
Northwich
Chester
Middlewich
Hurleston
Barbridge
Harecastle
Audlem
Trent & Mersey Canal
Etruria
Stoke-on-Trent
Market Drayton
Shropshire Union Canal
Stone
Gt Haywood
Norbury Jnct
Penkridge
Fradley
Gnosall
Hatherton
Huddlesford
Wheaton Aston
Autherley
Walsall
Wolverhampton
Birmingham Canal Navigations
BIRMINGHAM
Staffs & Worcs
Stourton
Coombeswood
Kidderminster
Stourport

covered with a white mantle of snow. It had come down heavily enough in the night to have covered everything to a depth of an inch or so. Snow, even in small quantities, invariably creates havoc on our roads and railways but makes not the slightest difference to the operation of inland waterways craft. As we made our way north, a good fire under the steerer's feet and our bellies full of hot porridge, it continued to fall lightly out of a windless sky.

Chillington's snow-covered woods were a pretty sight and the village at Brewood looked like something out of a Christmas card. Giving Jim the tiller, Ray and I swept the snow off the floorboards, lifted them up and propped them against the sides of the hold, with the top surface innermost so as to keep it dry. Below Wheaton Aston, Jim dropped off onto a pair of uphill boats which would take him back to Wolverhampton. We had to go some way past Knighton to turn in a more than usually silted up winding hole and were glad to get tied up under the canopy of the wharf which protected us from the weather.

The first job in the morning was to re-lay the false floors which were then covered with empty bags to protect the valuable cargo. We loaded about 18 tons, crumb being a bulky cargo, and clothed up, struggling with iron-hard frozen canvas and strings. Our top cloths were so old and thin that you could see daylight through them but they kept the weather out. As soon as we were well underway, one of us got into the hold, undid the top of a bag and extracted a quantity of crumb. It was delicious and, in those days of a restricted sweet ration, a welcome treat; but crumb, like any form of chocolate, has a laxative effect and we had to pay for our greed. Some of the crumb we grated up and used to make a chocolate drink.

That night we tied at the bottom of 'Hampton, arriving at Bournville about two the next afternoon, being unloaded right away. The narrowness of a Josher's gunwhales has been mentioned before: I was working my way along the outside of the boat unthreading the top-strings through their rings, for we didn't want them to fall in the water and get wet, when I slipped and fell in the cut. It was surprising that this didn't happen more often as, with both feet on a surface only about an inch wide, one hand was used to get a tenuous grip of the top planks (still covered with the cloths) while the other eased the string carefully through the ring, taking care to keep it dry.

I had to swim to the counter before I could manage to haul myself aboard. Fortunately we had such a good fire going in the cabin that getting out of my wet clothes and into dry wasn't too unpleasant. We spent the evening at Bournville, taking a Cotteridge tram to Breedon Cross to go to the pictures.

Off early next morning, we had to go to Breedon Cross again, the nearest winding-hole being at the former Midland Railway wharf there. Calling in at Sherborne Street for orders we were told to go immediately to Coombeswood to load tubes from the Stewarts & Lloyds works there. It was one of those frosty, sunny mornings which make you feel especially glad to be alive. The air was like wine. Never having been 'back of the map' before, the prospect of exploring a new canal was exciting and we were also feeling pleased that we had a back load, which meant more money. There was very little back loading on the Shropshire Union. Apart from tubes, an occasional boat would be sent to Bayliss, Jones and Bayliss to load nuts and bolts. Their factory was at Monmore Green and most of their traffic was despatched to the nearby railway basin in their own open boats, the motive power being a boatman with a shaft. A little cocoa residue from Bournville also moved to the Mersey Ports while the Knighton boats often returned with another raw material from Bournville called 'mast'.

Knowing that we had to go through the low Gosty Hill Tunnel, we took our cratch down while going along the Bottom Summit. By about 11.30 we were turning off to the left at Dudley Port. Exchanging greetings with the toll collector at Tividale Stop, we plunged into the long and spacious Netherton Tunnel with its towpaths on each side. This tunnel was unique in being lit, albeit dimly, by electric light. This was railway-boat territory and we encountered several of these craft in the tunnel, each carrying a flare at the fore-end and with its towline shortened to keep the horse in sight.

These were mostly iron open boats, their cargoes protected only by a tarpaulin flung over them in the hold, but a few ex-Shropshire Union wooden boats with cabins remained. Two I particularly remember were *Governor* and *Hogarth*. They ran from railway basins at Bloomfield (on the Wednesbury Oak Loop line), Tipton (Watery Lane) and Albion, to various destinations in Great Western territory west of the Dudley Ridge. There was, for instance, a boatage depot at the top of Delph Locks at Brierley Hill. Outward cargoes were often parcels of steel but, coming back, they might be full of wheelbarrows or dustbins, or piled high with crates of glass or pottery. *Hogarth*, which was based at Albion, was a regular 'crate boat' and very fine she looked in her black and white livery.

At Windmill End, we again branched off to the left, passing a railway basin, the Doulton pottery at Darby End and the arm where Rowley Rag stone used to be loaded, to pursue a sinuous course to the Old Hill entrance of Gosty Hill Tunnel. Here we had to wait for some boats to emerge, one of which turned out to be that of our erstwhile friend and mentor, Arthur Harris.

The scene which met our eyes at the far end of the tunnel was unexpected. There were literally dozens of boats at Coombeswood. Apart from a couple of Joshers, and the Joey boats which brought coal from Holly Bank and Cannock, coal was being loaded into boats on the towpath side to be pushed across to the works and many open boats loaded with tubes were to be seen working the short distance to Hawne railway basin. Some of these belonged to BR (Western Region) and to Thos. Bantock.

Following the other Joshers into the length, we were swiftly loaded with 15 tons of tubes and set off straight away on our return journey, arriving back in 'Hampton at about 6 pm after another exhilarating after dark run round the 'Hampton Pound.

When we got to the bottom of Audlem it was to find the cut completely blocked by a number of tube laden boats so we had, perforce, to stop as well. About 10pm when everyone had gone to bed, the *Clematis*, captained by Charlie Atkins Jnr., came down and insisted on all the boats being 'squared-up' so that he could get past. After much shafting and struggling, for none of the boats was properly tied up, he succeeded in getting his light 10 ton load through, carrying on through the night to pip the lot of us.

Just as we were congratulating ourselves on a successful trip, disaster struck. Going down the Weaver, I was in the cabin when the engine stopped. Before I could get outside there was an almighty crash. Flung to the far end of the cabin, I thought, for a moment, that the stove was going to come down on top of me. Fortunately its mountings held and I scrambled out.

Ray stood on the counter nursing his jaw. On entering Dutton Lock the engine had failed to reverse. There being no rope handy to throw up onto the lockside, there was nothing to stop our 30 tons of boat and cargo from colliding with the bottom gates. It says much for their sturdy construction that boat and gates were unharmed. Ray had continued to 'play with the rods' after the engine had 'gone out' and had had his chin level with the front surround of the cabin slide when she struck. He had sustained a broken jaw. The boat must have been moving very fast.

Making my injured captain comfortable in the cabin, I re-started the engine and took over for the last stretch down to Weston, meeting one of the powerful ex Bridgewater tugs in the flood lock, all the gates of which were, as usual, open. He didn't ease down and put a solid wave of water over our bows, our cratch not having been re-erected. When we got tied up at Weston, Ray went off to hospital in Liverpool where he had to spend three days.

The incident served to emphasise that, no matter how reliable a Bolinder was on reverse, there was always a chance that it would let you down, and that it was at all times vital to be prepared to bring up using a rope.

Unloading was immediate and, as there was plenty of metal waiting to go up, I soon had 20 tons of spelter in *Eagle*. Ray duly returned, his jaw as good as new, but we couldn't go up Weaver as the river was in flood and the management would not pay the Bridgewater tolls so that we could go via Runcorn Locks and Preston Brook.

To pass the time, Ray and I took the bus to Northwich where we found Bill and Flo Wain, with *Arabia* high in the air on the slip at the Waterways yard. Going over to Broken Cross, who should we come across but our erstwhile mate Bob Pettifer, now captain of the *Dunstan*. This was one of the Woolwich built, ex-Grand Union, boats with an extra deep hold. John Knill had had coamings built around the hold and equipped it with hatch covers instead of the usual planks, stands, side and top-cloths.

This was an ideal arrangement for one of these boats and had many advantages. Gone was the task of putting up and taking down the cratch every trip, and, the hold being covered when the boat was empty, it was always dry. BW obviously appreciated this as Bob seemed to get, mainly, cargoes of soda. The crew's work in covering the cargo was made much easier, and having to run from one end the other along the narrow top planks was a thing of the past.

It was a pity that, when this boat was eventually sold to John Walley, it was found that the coaming made it too difficult to shovel out coal so it had to be removed; but *Dunstan* deserves to be remembered as a successful attempt to improve on traditional practice in the carriage of general merchandise.

Among the boats tied up at Weston was the *Perch*, coincidence seeming to throw us frequently into Arthur's company. Arthur, who was known as 'Teena' or 'Brunjie', had had an interesting life. Born of a Gloucester boating family, he had worked with his father for the Severn and Canal Carrying Co. until the war, when he had been conscripted as a Bevin Boy and sent to work in the mines. A subsequent shortage of boatmen in the North-West resulted in his being drafted to the Mersey, Weaver Company, to work on an entirely unfamiliar canal. Returning to Gloucester where he married his wife, Winnie, he took over a Tree class motor and was one of the last narrowboatmen to work out of that port. Severn and Canal had only a few boats operating by the time they were nationalised and British Waterways soon stopped those. In 1949 Arthur and his boat were transferred to the North Western Division where he changed to the *Brill* (A wooden 9 hp boat) and later had the *Perch*. Although the Tree class boats were excellent carriers, being easily able to bring 23ton loads up the Shropshire Union, they didn't last long in the North West. In the Trees, the cabin was located in front of the engine-hole and this was an unpopular arrangement; as soon as they could, the boatmen changed into Josher boats.

Arthur was the epitome of the smart young boatman, his boat a model of tidiness. He would always don a pair of overalls to go into the engine-hole (Severners called it the engine room), removing them when he had finished. He had the 'survivor' mentality common on the cut and we had already found out, to our cost, that he would stop at nothing to gain a turn. Quite ruthless where money was concerned, he once persuaded us to pay 3/6d for a bag of coal which turned out to contain quite a bit of slack!

I got to know Arthur well and it has been a friendship that has lasted to this day. Both now armchair boatmen, we always manage to cover an amazing mileage when we meet, reliving our adventures on the cut.

A hard frost set in, cutting the flood levels on the Weaver and enabling the boats to proceed. Above Wardle Lock, we were breaking thick ice in company with Bill Keen who had the *Cormorant* and *Hilda*. The ice kept bringing us to a stand, and, when we tried to set back for a run at it, our engine kept going out on reverse. Bill, who, though big and rather fierce looking, was one of the nicest men you could wish to meet, came aboard to help us put it right.

This had to be done by adjusting the regulator spring for the reverse fuel pump. It will be appreciated that in order to confirm that the correct setting has been achieved, it is necessary to try and reverse the engine; but, until it has been adjusted exactly, the engine will continue to stop on reverse, unless, of course, it continues to run forward. So, although the adjustment is simple, to get it right is a matter of trial and error and can take a long time and require numerous restarts of the engine.

For some reason *Eagle's* engine now became difficult to start. Ray having no success, I had a go but had to resort to the practice of kicking backwards (not too hard) against the compression, keeping my foot on the pin, and using the added impetus for a strong forward kick. With our reverse back on form we struggled on at a snail's pace, ice crackling and groaning around us, to reach Barbridge where, in company with a number of other boats we tied up to await the icebreaker.

Teena was among our number, as was a noted North Western character of the day known as 'Mopstrangler'. He had acquired this nickname from an obsessive habit of continually mopping off his boat. Even passing another boat seemed to be enough to contaminate his and he would be seen disappearing into the distance vigorously wielding his mop. When he left the Shropshire Union to work on a 'steamer' on London River there was much speculation among the boatmen as to the length of mop handle he would need on his new craft.

While iced-up at Barbridge *Eagle* and I parted company. The circumstances are now all water under the bridge, Ray and I soon became friends again and have been so for many years, Teena invited me to ride up the cut with him on *Perch* until we met a friend of his who, he said, needed a mate. So once again my career on the cut took a new direction and I waited impatiently for the advent of the icebreaker.

CHAPTER NINE

HARD TIMES

·

The ice-breaker arrived next day and a crowd of boats started up and followed in its wake, not without difficulty as it was not one of those ice-boats that is rocked from side to side by a gang of men, thus breaking up the ice right across the canal. It merely cut a channel of its own width and, as it was shorter than a carrying boat, we had a job to follow it round the bends between Barbridge and Nantwich; but it was already starting to thaw and a miserable rain had set in.

Perch boasted a 'rain-shed', a set of wooden panels covered with canvas which hooked together to form a shelter over the top of the slide. The canvas hung down at the back to protect the steerer from behind and there was a small glass panel in the front. We were, therefore, completely warm and dry except when working the locks. This was the first Pup engine I had handled and the relatively high revs seemed strange after *Eagle*. She also had a fore-cabin and I had my one and only experience of sleeping in one of those tiny cubby-holes on our first night out of Barbridge. Containing only a miniature stove and a narrow cross-bed, it was cramped but cosy.

At Adderley we met Arthur's mate, Don, who also had a Fish Class, fore-cabined boat, the *Mullet*. I didn't know him, but remembered seeing him with the Tree Class motor with which he had been transferred from the South-Western Division. I changed my tack over and set off again northbound for Runcorn where we loaded Tripoli powder for Sherborne Street.

My new captain had been one of those involved in the Great Copper Fiddle and, on the way back to Birmingham, we had to tie up at Cox's Bank for a day for him to attend court. There was a pair of boats tied up there with us and some more boats back at Audlem Town Lock, most of the rest of the fleet being immobilised at various other places. The captain of the boats tied up in front of us had gone to

Court, taking his wife with him and leaving their numerous progeny on board. Mim Wilson, whose boats were at Audlem, appeared on the scene and we went aboard to visit the teenage daughter who was a friend of hers. The cabin was unbelievably squalid, seemingly crammed with pale looking children ranging in age from a baby to the daughter who was, I suppose, about 13. The tiny, overheated space stank of urine. This was my first real encounter with the more wretched side of family boating. How could a woman, who also had to help her husband work a pair of boats, cope with such a large family in these conditions? When they grew up and escaped the overcrowding, these children would be as clean and smart as anyone else. It was not their fault they were dirty, but that of poverty allied to cramped living conditions.

Encounters such as this led me to believe that the family boat system is not, as many enthusiasts would claim, ideal for working canal coats. There can be no objection to older children working on a canal boat but it is no place for smaller ones. Apart from the domestic difficulties, the risk of accident or drowning is ever present, a constant source of worry to already harrassed mothers. I wondered if any of those enthusiasts had ever seen, as I have, boat people desperately searching for a lost child, their faces grey with anxiety lest it had fallen in the cut. None of us having any comics, Mim and her friend engaged in a favourite pursuit of boat girls, that of doing up their hair. I was called upon to supply some Brylcream to assist the operation.

It was a crestfallen company of boatmen who returned, that evening, from Nantwich, most of them with £20 fines to pay; as so many had been involved there was no question of anyone being sacked. With the morning, we continued our journey south in miserable weather, pausing at Wheaton Aston to pinch some coal from the steam crane which unloaded dredgings there. My mate spied a brass wheel on one of the boiler mountings which he unscrewed and substituted for our iron speed-wheel. Not making very good progress, we were locked out at the bottom of 'Hampton and spent Christmas Day there. We walked up to the Top Lock where I encountered Jim Beady. After visiting friends on some of the many boats tied up there, he came back down to *Mullet* with me and stayed the night. As ours was the only boat at the bottom of 'Hampton, and Don had gone off somewhere I was very glad of his company.

Tripolo was one of the more messy cargoes we carried and the hold had to be given a good clean to remove any traces of the white powder.

Mixed with methylated spirits, this makes a good metal polish. Oiling up back at Albion Wharf, we came across two more of the many characters to be found on the Northern Road. The first was 'Charlie', a very dirty swan who made his home at Albion Wharf, contentedly living on scraps from the boats and drinking the chemical soup which passed for water in the 'Hampton Pound without any apparent ill effects. The other was Gilbert, a single-handed boatman who, in his usual inebriated state, was being helped onto his boat, after which someone kicked off his engine, untied the ropes and he happily sailed away. It usually took him about a fortnight to do a trip as he didn't reckon to work while he had money to stay in the pub.

Our orders were to go straight down and load spelter at Weston. *Mullet* was a much better swimming boat than *Eagle* and I thought that her fore-cabin added a touch of distinction to her lines; but her 9 hp engine simply refused to reverse. Don had a piece of string attached to the arm carrying the 'tables', a pull on which was supposed to actuate the reversing pump at the crucial moment, but, while I was on her, he used to reverse her in the engine-hole while I steered.

At 15 shillings a trip, plus food, I wasn't making much money, and *Mullet* was even more spartan than *Eagle*, so, while we were at Sherborne Street, I jumped at the chance to join a very smart pair of boats which were noted for the speed with which they got about the cut; the wages to be 30 shillings per trip with an additional 10 shillings if we went down with a back load.

We had to wait a couple of days for the motor to come off Saltley Dock where she had to go to have a new propellor put on. This had fallen off in one of the Shropshire Union bridgeholes but her captain subsequently recovered it and could boast, that trip, that he had two sets of blades.

There is no winding hole at Saltley so, as we were facing downhill, the boat having arrived via Digbeth and Bordesley, we had to return via Salford Junction. Saltley Dock is in the bottom pound of Saltley Locks and the section from there to Salford Bridge was a hive of activity, starting with the vast gasworks on either side, tar boats being loaded at Nechells up an arm on the towpath side. Next came Brotherton's Chemical Works followed by Saltley sidings, where coal was transhipped from railway wagons to boats for local delivery.

As we approached, a grimy face peered over the top of a coal wagon. It was none other than my friend, Joe, who I had last seen at Bodymoor Heath, now busily engaged in loading an Element's boat for the Premier Works above Saltley Locks. The same horse stood patiently waiting on the towpath. There was nobody about so we stopped and asked if we could have a bag of nuts. "It's coal fer 'ole round 'ere, y'know," said Joe, rudely. "But ah do' fancy yo' two so 'elp yerself." "Good job it ai' slack, then." laughed my mate. These cryptic remarks referred to an old boatman's saying, common on the BCN and Worcester & Birmingham Canals, which went back to the poverty stricken days of the 1930's, when women would exchange sexual favours for a supply of coal. I had been told that the custom had not entirely died out! Hence "Coal fer 'ole!" a remark which the more vulgar boatmen often parried with, "An' slack fer arse-'ole!"

Slack there was in plenty at the enormous Nechells Power Station a little further on, where many British Electricity Authority (as it was then titled) boats waited to go beneath the grabs. These were always known as Corporation boats in memory of their former municipal ownership, and, after we had negotiated Saltley 'Shallow' Lock, with its fall of only a few inches, we passed the Corporation Dock where they were maintained, before coming to Salford Junction and turning off for the long slog up the Eleven and the Thirteen.

Re-united with our butty at Sherborne Street, I was given the motor's tiller for the run to 'Hampton, and feeling very proud at being in charge of such a smart pair of boats, I enjoyed an exhilarating dash round the 'Hampton Pound in the dark, being congratulated on arrival for not having touched anywhere. I was soon to learn that I was working with a very particular couple who didn't approve of even the slightest scrape between the boats and the side of bridge-holes.

My new quarters were luxurious by comparison with *Eagle* and *Mullet*. The motor's cabin had a gleaming range and was adorned with brasswork, curtains and hanging-up plates. Best of all it had a feather bed with sheets. I spent a lot of time keeping everything shining.

While waiting for orders I helped Harry Barry down the locks, not because he needed any help as he now had only the single motor, but for something to do. As I have mentioned before, the Barrys were a very kind couple who would give you their last slice of bread. They were also real characters. Mrs Barry was heavily tattooed, it was whispered "all over", while Harry had worked in the Merchant Navy and was wont to describe, in minute detail, the procedure for starting up the ship's engines. They were both heavy smokers, and, although being an otherwise devoted couple, would keep their cigarette supplies secret. Harry might light up and say "Don't tell my missus I've got any," and you might get the same instruction from Elizabeth half an hour later.

In order to sustain their appetite for tobacco, they were in the habit of selling their rations, living mainly off porridge, and condensed milk sandwiches. The joke about a boater's breakfast being a cup of tea and a Woodbine might have been tailor-made for the Barrys.

After a day or two at the Top Lock we had orders to load tubes and we untied and went to spend the night at Coombeswood where the odd sack of DS nuts was added to our coal supplies. Approaching 'Hampton on the way back, I got on my bike and went ahead to get a horse out, having it ready on the lock-side by the time the boats arrived. Charlie said he would "drive and draw" for the butty, leaving me to take the motor down single-handed. This was the first time I had worked a motor down 'Hampton by myself and I was proud of my gleaming charge. Drawing a paddle behind the butty, I filled the top lock, opened the gate and stepped onto the counter, conscious of the appraising eyes from several moored boats. In with the clutch, on with the speed and a good touch of oil-rod to get her moving into the lock, before shutting off, de-clutching and stepping off to take a couple of nonchalant turns with the strap. Tying the boat down to the bottom gates with the tack string, I drew a paddle and ran down to the next lock. Top paddle up, bottom gates shut with a crash, up with the other top paddles, open the gate and run back to the lock above. Untying the tack string and draping it across the cratch, I kicked open the outside gate, pushed open the inside, jumped down onto the counter via the cabin top and accelerated out.

Repeating the procedure and running about at the double, I was at the bottom of the thick before I met Charlie coming back with the horse. Seeing me coming he had filled the next lock. You couldn't fill too many in front as an uphill boat might turn up. We changed over and I took the horse back to its stable, taking my bike with me. A speedy ride down the locks followed and I caught our boats up at the Cut End. That night we went to Norbury and from there to Weston, loaded copper cathodes and met the rest of the tube consignment, still on their way down, at Middlewich. Charlie was in high good humour at the speed with which we had got down, emptied and reloaded.

The routine we usually adopted when coming back up was to leave Weston at 7 am, when the swing-bridge opened, and go to Barbridge.

The next day's work was to Norbury and thence into Birmingham unless it was a Sunday when we would, of course, find Wolverhampton Locks shut and have to tie up around midday. To persist, in these days of lighter traffic and, consequently, less use of water, in the old custom of closing 'Hampton from early Saturday afternoon to Monday morning with all the resulting delays to craft, seemed to me to be the height of folly; and in fact the practice was to be later abandoned.

Working to the above routine meant that, even in the middle of winter, we were able to work nearly all the locks in daylight, Chumston and Tipton Factory being the exception. Another advantage was that Barbridge and Norbury were among the very few places on the Shropshire Union where a loaded boat could be tied up properly against the side. This could also be done at Audlem Town Wharf and at Knighton, but at other stopping places such as above Wardle Lock, Cox's Bank, Nantwich and Gnosall you were "tied up in the middle of the cut." It was no joke, at the end of a long day's work, struggling, perhaps in the freezing cold or in pouring rain, to secure a pair of boats when you couldn't get anywhere near the bank.

Having now been boating for a year, I had become hardened to the work and was quite unaffected by the long hours and bad weather. Although we worked much faster than *Columba* and *Uranus* had done, life was easier with a properly planned routine and our long tow-rope cut out a lot of bowhauling. Nevertheless, the three narrow locks at Middlewich, the two at Hack Green and the flights of five each at Adderley and Drayton all meant getting the rope over your shoulder, a job which fell to me. Most of the rest of the time I spent on the motor's footboard. Our butty was an ex-Grand Union boat identical to *Uranus* but we used to put a much heavier load on her making her harder to bowhaul.

One stretch where I didn't usually steer the motor was going up the Weaver with its heavy traffic and locks that necessitated reversing; but that first trip, Charlie wasn't feeling too well and gave her to me in Dutton Lock. I was scared stiff in case I missed reverse at Saltersford, as, strangely enough, I had only needed to reverse her on one previous occasion. All went well but I was relieved when a recovered Charlie took over again for the stretch to the Lift. Actually, our motor was very reliable on reverse and was unusual in preferring the clutch to be left in when manoeuvring.

In midwinter, darkness would fall while we were in the Minshull Pound, and it was along here that my inexperience showed itself. The

Shropshire Union had not, as yet, had much attention from the new draglines. Apart from a stretch near Betton Wood and another north of Cut End, it remained as mud encumbered as when I had first worked on it. Although the Middlewich Branch may give the impression of being straight, there are, in fact, some subtle changes of channel. Sometimes, if I was on our heavily loaded butty in the dark, I would allow the boat to scrape the bottom. Although I was not aware of being out of the channel, it could be clearly heard in the cabin even though the bottom was only soft mud. When this happened I would be berated in no uncertain terms.

The narrow SU bridge-holes sometimes got me into trouble. Unlike those on most canals, the channel beneath them was only just wide enough to admit a boat, and this, combined with the accumulation of mud that had been pushed by loaded boats into their approaches, meant that speed had to be reduced to a minimum when quite a long distance away. We used to reckon about two telegraph poles' length. In my early days with John Knill, all of us often failed to shut off early enough with the result that the motor would stop and the butty would rush up and clout her stern. My technique had improved with practice but shutting off even a little too late could add time to the overall journey and I was often in trouble for "driving in the bridges". My employers were obsessed with saving minutes and would shout "keep her straight!" from the butty if I allowed the motor to wander even a little.

The unconsciously slap-happy style of boating of my former days now went for ever. Proper boating practices were to be so firmly impressed on me that they would serve me faithfully for the rest of my time on the cut.

The extremes of cabin decoration found on the London road were not practised "Down the North"; but most of us were sticklers for cleanliness and London boats would sometimes be referred to as "clean on top and dirty underneath". Southerners would retaliate with this rhyme:

"The Shropshire Union coat of arms
Is an upturned tiller and an empty starn,
A ragged mop and a knotted line.
Don't our Shropshire Union shine!"

"Upturned tiller" meant that a boat spent much of its time tied up and "empty starn" referred to the food cupboard.

Another rhyme often recited was:

"Come all you jolly boatmen who want a job a-flying.
Just step aboard the (name of boat) 'cos all the crew are dying.
The Captain's dying of hunger,
The mate is dying of thirst,
An' the Missus can't get off to the locks
Because her shoes have burst."

This seems to be a parody of the better known "Flyboat Song" which exhorts a young man to go and work on the steam flyboats of old.

Arriving back at Wolverhampton after emptying at Sherborne Street, we were treated to the unusual sight of a Josher unloading in the LMR railway basin. The boat was the *Eagle*, Ray having come up with a load of bentonite clay for which, presumably, BW had no spare warehousing space. As the "Stourlifters" had ceased to run some months previously, this may well have been the last boat to unload there as I never heard of any others doing so.

On the way down we encountered several boats tied up in out of the way places while their captains struggled to get their engines going. Diesel oil for the Northern Joshers was stored in a large tank at Albion Wharf which was replenished by Thos. Clayton oil boats from Ellesmere Port. Apparently a cargo with a lot of water in it had been delivered and several boats had been re-fuelled with this before the contamination was discovered, causing many engine failures.

Our butty's 'elum was pretty shaky due to the wood having rotted and we had to go to the BW dock at Northwich where they made us a new one. The dock, which had formerly belonged to the Weaver Navigation Co., wasn't accustomed to this kind of work and it took several days to make. It was interesting to watch a construction involving such large and heavy pieces of wood. The 'elum seemed all right when it was finished and painted but, when hung on the boat, it looked terrible, the tingles sloping downwards away from the ram's head instead of being level or rising very slightly.

Ken and Vern Nixon had to pay a visit to the dock while we were there and the three of us paddled across the river in a small square maintenance flat with sides only a few inches high. In the middle of the pitch dark river, Ken and Vern started rocking the tiny craft. This didn't amuse me one bit; I could swim, but knew that they couldn't, and I didn't fancy floundering in the icy water with two large and helpless non-swimmers for company.

The delay on the dock was followed by a very slack time for traffic. Eventually we got a load of spelter for Birmingham. On this occasion we started very early in the morning from 'Hampton in a heavy fog, quite the worst one I had experienced since I had been on the cut. Considering the frequency of fogs in those days of severe air pollution, I had been lucky. This one was a really pea-souper and couldn't have happened in a worse place with all the sharp bends and awkward bridgeholes to contend with. Much of the boatman's art consists in knowing the cut in minute detail. Not surprisingly, my knowledge was not that intensive, but it was assumed to be and I was given the butty's tiller and expected to get on with it. It was nerve-wracking. The ghostly shapes of bridgeholes and landmarks would loom suddenly up in front of me and I would row frantically at the tiller to avoid hitting anything. I was beginning to relax a little when we had cleared Hickman's as the cut is fairly straight from here onwards, when suddenly there was an almighty crash and the boat heeled alarmingly to the clatter of pots, pans and hanging-up plates. There was a squeal of feminine fury from below and I was ignominiously relieved from my post until the fog lifted. At the Tipton end of the steelworks was a demolished bridge. I had forgotten about this and had collided with the towpath where it projected out into the cut under the old bridgehole. The trouble with working as a mate to experienced boat people was that they often took the knowledge acquired during a lifetime's boating for granted and expected you to be just as capable.

Although I still got a lot of satisfaction from boating, I endured nagging feelings of insecurity. Traffic was so scarce that many weeks we only earned the fall-back of £2 10s per boat and this not only meant that my earnings were extremely small but that it was becoming evident that, unless there was improvement in trade, my employers wouldn't be able to keep me on, as the cost of my food was a substantial slice of their wages. The whole idea of employing a mate was to relieve them of some of their work and, if the boats spent most of their time tied up, there was not much point in incurring this expense.

Despite the difficulties and hardships, I was determined to stick it out until I could get a single motor. How I envied those fortunate single-handed boatmen, able to gaze contentedly at the world from their footboards, calling no man master and free to take a day off, or work all night, just as the mood suited them. Such independence seemed to me then, as it still does now, a pearl beyond price.

I was now just coming up to my eighteenth birthday, and, taking my courage in both hands, for I was a far from confident youth, I went into the office and raised the matter with Dick Tart who was then in charge at Wolverhampton. He readily assented to my request, telling me that a certain boatman had just given his trip's notice and that I could have his boat when he turned it up. I was still in the office when the second post came and was just going out of the door when I was called back. "Hang on, Tom, there's one for you." It was a buff envelope marked OHMS. My heart sank. I knew what it was although I had hoped that I would be somehow overlooked. Ripping it open, my worst fears were confirmed as I read the instruction to register for National Service.

A date a few weeks hence was given. There was nothing else to do but slog on, and way we went down the cut to load polythene powder at Weston for Norbury, whence it would be delivered by road to Wellington. Several other boats also loaded this traffic including Joe Hollinshead, who we called 'Charcoal'. I remember this because he wanted to apply for a pair of Cowpars and, being a "scholard", I was asked to write a letter for him.

Several days were spent at Norbury and I was down to my last penny by the time we were sent to Anderton for orders. Here we were told to go down the Lift and put in two loads of packet soda at the ICI works, one for Wolverhampton and one for Birmingham (Bridge St.). After a very early start from above the Lift, we were going up Audlem in the late afternoon when I got into difficulty with the horse. I had driven this animal up and down Audlem Locks many times and always found it very amenable and easy to handle. About halfway up the flight there is a bridgehole immediately above one of the locks. The boat cross-winded in the lock tail, which stopped it, and the horse, quite sensibly, baulked at starting it again while he was on the slippery brickwork under the bridge. Eventually the Missus got off the boat, came up on the lock side and tried to get the horse to pull. By now thoroughly nervous, it turned round and reared up, front legs flailing. Without turning a hair, the woman, who was about five feet nothing in height, stepped up to it and hit it hard on the nose with her fist. She had to do that several times before the animal quietened and then the line had to be shortened so that the horse was pulling before it entered the bridge. Only then would it re-start the boat. Naturally I got told off for not being able to cope with the situation.

Stopping at Cox's Bank, we made Wheaton Aston the next night, going up the locks and emptying one boat the following day. I didn't accompany our boats into Birmingham as this was the day I had to register, and presenting myself at the appointed time and place, I was given a series of tests and told that I would be a Clerk (Equipment Accounting) in the RAF. I would have preferred the Air/Sea Rescue Branch but it was necessary to sign on for ten years to get into that. Because the pay would be more, I decided to sign on for three years instead of the obligatory two.

After lunch at the British Restaurant, one of those cheap eating places instituted by the Government during the war, I looked in at the Top Lock. Here I fell in with a couple who worked a pair of Claytons and whose mate had just been called up. As the firm required them to have a minimum crew of three, they offered me the job. This would have suited me fine as these oil boats worked continuously, being required to complete each return trip between Ellesmere Port and Oldbury within a week. But the offer had come too late and I had to regretfully explain the position. However, to save me travelling to Birmingham I was invited to spend the night aboard and the fat, jolly wife of the captain took myself and their mate to the local music hall for the evening.

Having completed the formalities of registering, I decided to go home for a few days before my actual joining date; but first I needed the fare as my parents now lived in Southsea. To get the required amount I would have to cash some Savings Certificates which, I found, would take three days. The pair of boats on which I had been working had gone down the cut so this meant that I had to hang around 'Hampton for two more nights. The next day I had a five shilling hobble which enabled me to buy some food, but there were no boatmen I knew at the Top Lock and somehow it never occurred to me to ask Jim to put me up, so I decided to sleep out. I selected a suitable spot under the wide railway bridge which crosses the cut between Cut End and the bottom of 'Hampton Locks. Snow had fallen but it wasn't particularly cold and the ground was no harder than *Eagle's* side-bed. Nevertheless it was an experience I was glad to never have to repeat.

The following afternoon I hobbled the *Rudd* down 'Hampton, being given the exceptional sum of seven and sixpence! Her captain, who had not long taken her on, was a pleasant youth little older than myself. He asked me if I would like to do a few trips with him but it was now too late for any more boating. However I agreed to steer as far as Brewood, while he cooked his tea and shared it between us.

And so, just as on my first trip to the North, I came to Cut End in the twilight of a winter's day; and the magic was still there as I took the tiller and headed off into that mysterious Shropshire Union country of field and covert, valley and rocking. Below me, in the cabin, the soft lamplight glowed and the range was warm to my feet. An owl hooted and bright stars shone overhead, and I longed, with all the intensity of my eighteen year old being, to be heading northwards through the night, to find my personal nirvana in those lost and lonely reaches.

Mundane reality called, and I regretfully stepped ashore at Brewood and mounted my bike for the ride back to Wolverhampton where I now had enough money to pay for a bed for the night.

CHAPTER TEN

NUMBER ONE

H aving prised my savings out of the reluctant clutches of the Post Office, I made my way to Low Level station, and was soon being whirled southwards. My stay in Southsea was short as I had little money, so I wrote to the RAF and asked for my enlistment date to be advanced. A ticket to Wolverhampton arrived by return of post and I was off again, travelling up to London on one of the fast Portsmouth Electrics, and across the city by Underground to arrive at Paddington. With time to spare before my train, I walked up the road and had a look at the canal at Paddington Basin.

I had not lost my capacity to enjoy railway travel and this was my first night journey alone. Returning to the station, I thrilled to the atmosphere of the vaulted cavern, its dim lights throwing dark shadows on platform and concourse. Around me stood old friends, locomotives whose names had been familiar since boyhood, wreathed in steam, their footplates lit by open fire-box doors.

I was to travel on the Night Birkenhead Express, and, before joining the train, I walked up the platform to watch our engine being coupled on. As the grimy monster backed down onto our long rake of coaches, my spine tingled as I imagined her journey through the night, the driver leaning out of his cab intent on his signals, his mate feeding the insatiable fire with shovel after shovelful of coal, the 'ting' of block bells in the lonely boxes as the signalmen leant out to observe the tail lamp before sending "Train Out Of Section" and clearing their instruments.

I was wide awake and spent the journey peering out in search of familiar landmarks and watching the activity at the stations we stopped at. Finally, in the early hours of the morning, we drew up at Wolverhampton. A few hours later I joined the group of recruits with whom I was to travel and was on the train again, this time a London

Midland one, bound for Cardington in Bedfordshire.

I had not looked forward to the prospect of National Service with any enjoyment; but that afternoon, after taking the oath and settling down in the barrack hut, I was suddenly overcome with the most overwhelming feeling of relief, as though all the troubles of the world had been taken off my shoulders. For the next three years, I could rely on a regular pay packet and would be fed, clothed and housed. I would live a life of complete security, quite independent of the whims of those market forces we are told are so good for us. The insecurity of the last few months had been more of a strain on my still rather shy and diffident nature than I had realised.

Just how desperate things had become for me was demonstrated next morning when I was forced to borrow a shilling for my first Service hair cut. I made a mental resolution that I was never going to get in the same position again.

For a few days I determined never to return to the cut; but my very strong attachment to that way of life soon overcame these sentiments and the bad memories faded leaving only the good ones to be remembered. It had been a hard life, often bitter, but the worst was over. When I went back boating, it would be as a Captain and already I could see, in my mind's eye, myself working a smart boat, agleam with polished brass and scrubbed woodwork, briskly along the Midland canals, the professional equal of my former masters.

From Cardington I moved to Melksham in Wiltshire, close to the remains of the Wilts & Berks Canal. The eight week period of square-bashing I detested, although I put on some much needed weight; but I was sustained by news of the cut from several friends, particularly Jim Beady, who corresponded regularly with me throughout my RAF service.

Square-bashing was followed by my first leave during which I first visited an aunt and uncle in Bristol and then set off to Braunston where J.K. had invited me for a couple of days boating. I found him alone with *Columba* in which he had just had installed a twin cylinder Bolinder to replace that dreadful old National. This engine had a gearbox and compressed air starting and the hit and miss governor had gone but otherwise it was similar to the Bolinders I had been used to except that blowlamps, spindles and hot-bulbs were duplicated. Despite our joint efforts, we had enormous difficulty in starting this engine, for no obvious reason that I could see; it was to remain in *Columba* only a few years. We went to Sutton's, where I was pleased to find George and Sonia and also the Rogers. After an enjoyable evening in their company I stayed the night there before setting off to 'Hampton to visit Jim.

There was a crowd of boats at the Top Lock and I detected a subtle change in the attitude of the other boatmen. When I had been a mate many of the older Captains had looked upon me as a boy, but now, appearing on the towpath in my uniform, I sensed that I was being looked upon as an adult. Charlie was there and I went aboard for an hour or two before going round to Jim's to spend the night. British Waterways had just started to instal electric light in its Northern Fleet and Charlie was not pleased at the prospect. "If oil lamps were good enough fer my feyther, they'm good enough fer me," he remarked. "If anyone tries to put electric lights on my boats ah'll throw 'em in the cut."

Jim and I had much to talk about when he returned late from his long day on the Hednesford to Nechells coal boats. He had not yet made up his mind to go Joshering but was thinking of driving a brewery dray. This pleasant interlude over, it was back to Bristol to pick up my kit before proceeding to my new posting at Hendon.

Hendon was a much prized posting and I look back on my days there as among the happiest of my life. Clerical work in the RAF, I found, bore no resemblance to my hated insurance office in Reading. The atmosphere was relaxed, the company congenial, and our labours over invoice and ledger interspersed with lengthy tea breaks and games of penny-ha'penny football. Our office was a cosy hut, warmed in winter by a coke stove and right next to the perimeter fence separating us from the Midland main line which treated me to a constant procession of trains; Jubilees and Compounds flailing their way northwards, enormous coal trains creeping towards Brent Yard and sprightly suburban passengers. Right outside the camp gates was Colindale Station, from where, for the price of ninepence, the Northern Line would take you into London and back.

Not long after my arrival at Hendon, I heard from Ray White. He had given up the *Eagle* and was now working as a bus conductor. He and his girl-friend lived in a bed-sitter in Pimlico, where I regularly visited them to chat about old times. Often we would indulge in an hour or two's tram riding, a terminus of the moaning, clattering monsters being close to hand at Victoria.

I now had a girlfriend myself, a gorgeous red-head who lived near my uncle and aunt. Every four weeks, when I was entitled to a 48 hour pass, I would tear up to Paddington to catch the Bristol train. The fare (at Forces rate) was 24 shillings return.

Having few expenses, I was saving money, being able to supplement my two pounds, nine shillings a week wage by doing extra guard and fire picket duties for those of my mates who lived nearby and wanted to spend as much time as possible at home.

On other weekends we were allowed a 36 hour pass. One of my colleagues introduced me to the delights of dinghy sailing and we spent many happy hours on the nearby Welsh Harp reservoir; but my favourite diversion was to take a bus to Preston Road Station on the Metropolitan Line and head for the Grand Union Canal. At different times I covered the entire towpath from Berko to Brentford. The Metropolitan Line would take me to Uxbridge, Ricky or Croxley, and the London Midland Region farther afield. Sometimes I would come across *Columba* and *Uranus*, or *Cairo* and *Warwick*, and be able to keep my hand in with strap and windlass.

One unexpected encounter was on a visit to Brentford where I came across Bill and Flo Wain who were now working for Rayners. On another occasion I went to Woking and explored the Basingstoke Canal. But my favourite walk was between Uxbridge and Ricky. No matter how many times I went, there was always a twinge of excited anticipation when I got off the train at Uxbridge. Free from all worries for the first time since I had been a small child, I could saunter along the towpath with no nagging cares to intrude upon my enjoyment. Exchanging greetings with passing boats, pausing perhaps, to shut a gate for someone, I would walk steadily up the valley, arriving at Ricky in good time to enjoy a cup of tea and a sandwich before boarding the train for my return journey. It was at Ricky that I observed signs of hope for the future. Walkers Dock were building two butties for the North Western Division, the first new boats to be ordered by British Waterways; and at the new Colne Valley Sewerage Works a grab was being installed to unload coal brought by canal.

Sitting in the train on my way back from these expeditions, I would light up a contemplative cigarette and enjoy that strange, bitter-sweet, rather pleasant melancholy known only to the young, when one is temporarily deprived of some much desired object but fully expects to regain it before long.

As the winter of 1951 drew on, I heard from Mike and Polly Rogers, who were living at Crouch End, having converted *Mabel* into a passenger carrying hotel boat. I used to visit them once a fortnight and we would talk about boats and play Ludo. Sometimes I met George Smith there, he and Sonia having split up and left the boats. George now worked ashore and lodged nearby.

My idyllic life at Hendon was shattered by news of a posting to the Suez Canal Zone. Taking a reluctant farewell of my girlfriend and paying a final brief visit to 'Hampton, I set off for a transit camp near Preston before boarding the troop ship.

Of my two years in Egypt little need be said. With my bed space surrounded with pictures of boats rather than the more usual pin-ups, the highlights of my life were letters from my boating friends. Jim had finally taken the plunge and gone Joshering, and was having, as I had done, a hard time as a mate. But he was shortly to be called-up and had gone on the Northern Boats mainly to establish an entitlement to a single motor when he got demobbed. He was later sent to the Canal Zone where he worked on Z Craft at Port Said, but we never managed to meet because of the difficulties of travel.

Ray had returned to the cut with a pair of Barlow's and sent me regular and sometimes hilarious accounts of his adventures. From him, I learnt that North Western boats were now making trips through to the Grand Union, loading at Manchester and carrying grain to Northampton or Southall and timber to Old Ford. London boats were penetrating deep into the Black Country to load copper at Goscote on the Wyrley & Essington Canal.

When, in 1953, Ray took on a Charles Ballinger horse boat on the Worcester & Birmingham Canal, I had yet stranger tales to read, about backwoods of the BCN I had never even heard of, and Cannock, Walsall Wood and Ryders Green became familiar to me through his letters. There were several reports of Northern Joshers trading down to Worcester and Gloucester, the first British Waterways boats to do so since 1949.

Much talked about at the time was the decision by BW to dredge the northern part of the Stratford Canal, the completion of which work was marked by despatching six pairs of London boats to Stourport.

There was sad news too. The old established Anderton Company had sold out to Mersey-Weaver's and the high piled crate boats were to be seen no more. Cowpars tank boats had finished, while, on the Oxford, the important Wolvercote coal contract and tar from Oxford Gas Works had been lost from the canal.

In the autumn of 1953, with only five months of my service to complete, I had a letter from John Knill. Having bought the ex-Grand Union, Ricky motor *Hesperus*, he had now decided to sell it. Did I want it for £150? I had thought of applying for a motor in the North West when the happy day of demob finally arrived but, as yet, had made no firm plans. *Hesperus* was only seventeen years old and had not done a great deal of work, having spent several years as a house-boat. At the price she seemed a reasonable buy, even sight unseen, and John assured me that she could be put in first class trading order about as much again. With a boat of my own I could achieve the ultimate in independence. I would not be just a Captain but a Master Boatman, and I could indulge my taste for variety by 'following the trade' rather than being tied down to the Mersey-Birmingham route.

The thought of having my own place to live, to be able to shut the doors on the outside world, to work when, where, and how I liked, won the day. I put the cheque in the post and before long had the receipt. The remaining months of my service passed in a fever of impatience, but I was happy in the knowledge that *Hesperus* was mine and would be waiting for me as soon as I stepped off the train at Braunston.

The trials and tribulations of a canal boat mate were over. I was now a Number One.

GLOSSARY

Back-end	Section of hold immediately in front of cabin or engine room.
Barge	Flat bottomed vessel of at least 14 feet beam.
Big Engine	Josher fitted with a 15hp Bolinder. The custom of referring to powered craft as "Engines" began with the introduction of steamers.
Blades	Propellor. 'Bladefull' refers to a fouled prop.
Black Boats	Thos. Clayton boats used for short distance transport of bulk liquids on the BCN and adjoining canals; the crew not living aboard. The cabins were black, but it is not certain whether the name derives from this or from the usual cargo of gas tar.
Boatage depot	Waterside premises operated by a railway company, but to which there was no direct access by rail. Goods were moved between these depots and a convenient railway basin (q.v.) in boats operated by the railway or its agents, thereby enabling it to trade outside its own rail served territory.
Bottom End	The northern and, in respect of the level of the canal, lower end of the Warwickshire coalfield.
Bottom Road	Grand Union boatmen's term for the route from Birmingham to the Warwickshire coalfield via the Birmingham & Fazeley Canal – the 'Top Road' being via Braunston. Boatmen engaged on local work would refer to the B&F as the 'Old Cut' to distinguish it from the Tame Valley Canal, known as the 'New Cut'.
Buffer Depot	Government warehouse established to hold reserve supplies of food.
Butty	Boat working in company with another or, more specifically, one towed by a motor boat. 'To Butty': to travel in company with another boat.
Cratch	Tent shaped structure of wood and canvas at front of hold.

Cross-wind	To allow a boat to enter a lock or narrow place at an angle thus bringing it to a stop and possibly doing some damage.
Deckboard	Triangular board which may be part of cratch (in which case it is usually covered by the deckcloth) or may stand by itself supporting the front of the forward top plank, the rear end of which is supported by the mast. Often decorated.
Dolly	Small steel bollard on stern of motor boat.
Dry Side	Free board
'Elum'	Rudder
Flat	Merseyside term for barge. Mersey flats carried up to 100 tons and were able to navigate the Bridgewater, Rochdale and Sankey canals. The larger Weaver flats could carry up to 250 tons.
Flyboat	Canal boat operating night and day with an all male crew working in shifts.
Hatches	Small cockpit at stern of horse boat or butty.
Hold back	To go astern.
Hold in	To steer towards the towpath.
Hold out	To steer away from the towpath.
Joey Boat	Boatman's name for an unmotorised narrow boat without permanent living accommodation or provision for covering the cargo. Joey boats hauled by horses or tugs were mainly used on short distance journeys around Birmingham but occasionally went further afield. It has become common for these boats to be described as 'day boats' but the term is actually unknown to boatmen. The official description, used, for instance, on Gauging Tables, is 'open boat'; a boat which is fitted with permanent living accommodation being described as a cabin boat. These terms are, to some extent, misleading as most open boats had cabins and many cabin boats had open holds.
Josher	A boat belonging to the firm of Fellows, Morton and Clayton Ltd.
Knobstick	A boat belonging to the Anderton Company.
Looby	Spring loaded pin on top of a cabin boat's mast to which the towline is attached. If fouled it will fly off automatically.
Night Owl	A boatman in the habit of working at night.
Number One	An owner boatman.
Paddle	Valve for admitting water onto or out of lock, Ground paddles are situated on the lockside, gate paddles (or 'centres') in the gates. Side paddles control the flow of water to and from side-ponds or between the chambers of duplicate locks.

Peg (to)	To attach the towline to the horse's gear.
Preston Boat	Boat engaged in the Preston Brook trade.
Pup	9 hp Bolinder engine, or boat equipped with same.
Railway Boats	Boats operated by a railway company, its agents or customers between Railway Basins and the customers premises, directly or via Boatage Depots (q.v.) The term 'Station Boat' was more commonly used by boatmen.
Railway Basin	A basin designed and equipped for the direct transfer of goods between canal boat and railway wagon and vice versa. The railway basin at Chillington Road, Wolverhampton survives in its original state and could accommodate up to six boats at a time, being arranged so that cargoes to or from the outermost boat on one side of the basin could be moved, even if the inner berths were obstructed by wagons. Boatmen knew these basins as 'Station Arms'.
Rams Head	Wooden rudder post on a horse boat or butty.
Red Ticket	Authority for a boat with an urgent cargo to pass through locks when closed.
Rocking	Boatmens name for a cutting.
Rods	Controls of a Bolinder engine: e.g. "He knows how to handle the rods."
Runcorn Boat	A local design of narrow boat for use on the Bridgewater and adjacent canals.
Severner	Narrow boat of distinctive shape used on the river Severn and its tributary canals. More specifically a boat belonging to the Severn & Canal Carrying Co.
Side-pond	A chamber alongside a lock holding water at a level halfway between the upper and lower pounds. Used to half fill an empty lock and to receive water from a full lock until a level has been made, thus economising in the use of water.
Stourlifter	Railway boat operated by British Railways (London Midland Region) and its predecessors betwen Wolverhampton, Kidderminster and Stourport.
Strap (noun)	Rope used for checking a boat. (Except cross-straps used for towing an empty butty).
Strangle	To dry a rag mop by rolling the stick up and down your arm.
String	Much of the decorative rope work on a narrow boat is described as 'strings'. Where used for operating ropes, the term usually refers to those used for mooring or to secure something. Thus, fore-string, stern-string tiller-string, tack-string.
Swim	The progress of a boat through the water in terms of whether it is good or bad.

Tables	The planes over which move the regulator weights which operate the fuel and reverse pump plungers on a Bolinder. Boatmen liked to see the weights "Jumping over the tables".
Timberhead	Wooden bollard fitted to certain regional narrow boats.
Tingles	Horizontal pieces of wool strengthening an 'elum
Tipcate	Sausage shaped stern fender used on motorboats.
Valley	Boatmens name for an embankment.
Wind	To turn a boat.
Winding hole	Turning place in canal.
Woolwich Boat	Boats built at Harland and Wolf, Woolwich for the Grand Union Canal Carrying Co. Of recent years, writers have shown a tendency to treat canal boats like railway engines by putting them into 'name' classes. Unfortunately very few of these classes are sufficiently homogenous to justify such treatment. There are a few exceptions, for instance I have referred to the eight all welded motor boats built for the Severn and Canal Carrying Co. in 1935 as the Tree Class but this is a matter of convenience and not an authentic canal term. Boatmen would describe a boat by its size and builder e.g. small Woolwich, or its owner, e.g. Josher, or its function e.g. Station Boat. Regional descriptions were to be found like Severner, Runcorn Boat or Wiganer. The idea of classes of boat is quite foreign to boatmen although it does have a certain, albeit limited, convenience to writers. The trouble is when the idea is taken to absurd lengths as in the caption to a photo of three quite different horse boats which were described as 'Girl Class butties'. The number of firms and boatyards which owned or built boats with girl's names is very large indeed!

I N D E X

Titles of publications are shown in *italics*. 'C' indicates 'Canal'.
Boat names are shown in SMALL CAPITALS.